Colored Water:
Dixie Through Egyptian Eyes

A MEMOIR BY

ASHRAF EL-BAYOUMI

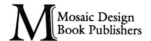
Mosaic Design
Book Publishers

Colored Water:
Dixie Through Egyptian Eyes

First Printing – September 2016

ISBN: 978-0-9968933-0-5 *(paperback)*
ISBN: 978-0-9968933-1-2 *(eBook)*

Printed in the United States of America on acid-free paper.

Published by Mosaic Design Book Publishers
Dearborn, Michigan USA

0 1 2 3 4 5 6 7 8 9

DEDICATION

To my family:
Soheir Morsy, my wife of 60 years;

Our children, Jehan, Mona (and her husband Fuad) and Amr;

Our grandchildren, Cherine, Ziad, Fairouz, Nadine and Yasmine.

And

To the memory of Dr. Michael Kasha,
my inspiring Ph.D. professor.

ACKNOWLEDGMENTS

From the start, this book became a family venture when interest was expressed in my reminiscing over dinner followed listing possible episodes with Soheir.

Special thanks to friends and family for their tremendous encouragement.

My appreciation is also offered to all of those who made my early years in the U.S. a fulfilling, enjoyable and valuable learning experience.

Cover photo: The author at home in Alexandria, 1954.
Back cover photo: The author in Luxor, 2015.

CONTENTS

EPISODE ONE:

From Iskendereya to Dixie: Floreeda, Here I Come!

On the Tram In Alexandria

Riding the tram in Iskendereya (Alexandria, Egypt) in the Fifties was a pleasurable experience, especially in first class. Seats were very comfortable, made of brown genuine leather. Conductors wore formal suits, dark blue in winter and olive green khaki in summer. They were generally polite and adequately educated. Several of them were fond of making creative musical sounds with their whistles at each stop. As a regular tram rider for four years, I knew most of them personally. On the tram I often met friends, relatives, and occasionally some of my university professors, most of whom used public transportation then. When that happened, I was obliged, out of respect, to offer my seat if none were available. Back then, the student-professor relationship was quite formal.

It was around March 1955, a few months after I was appointed a "moeid" (teaching assistant) in the Chemistry Department, thus crowning my four years of rigorous studies at the Faculty of Science at Alexandria University. In June of the previous year I had graduated with First Honors, which secured my appointment as a "moeid". I was the only one of my class to get such a prestigious position in the Chemistry Department. The position was permanent and thus the first step in the long track of becoming a university professor. In practice, a "moeid" is like being a tenured teaching assistant! Suddenly, I had many students, some of them even older than myself. They would offer me seats on the tram when the occasion arose. I must admit that it was gratifying to hear my name called out in the crowd: "Doct'oor Ashraf, please have my seat"! I had barely begun my Masters degree research, let alone doctorate training! First names, coupled with the title Doctor, or "Doc'toor", as we pronounce it in Arabic, were used to address both professors with a genuine doctorate and young teaching assistants with a pseudo doctorate. My pleasure was doubled when some of the passengers noticed the whole act: the seat offer, my initial polite decline, the persistence of the offer, my half-hearted reluctance, and finally my acceptance. Often, there were expressions of surprise at my being a "moeid", for I was only nineteen. My skinny figure gave me an even younger appearance.

The habit of using titles in Egypt was a part of the culture since the days of Turkish Ottoman rule. The king granted formal titles like "Beyk" and "Pasha", and just before the 1952 Revolution (which terminated King Farouk's rule) titles were granted for those who made generous donations that went directly to the King. In addition, a few individuals were granted special titles like "Saaheb Elmaaly" (the one who has the most elevated status). The less prestigious "Beyk" was used liberally, to address high post officials like my father, and sometimes, even not so high officials. In addressing a letter one used terms such as "Hadrat Saheb Elezzah" (you who have dignity) or "Hadrat Saheb Elsaada" (you who have happiness). The culture of "embroidered honorific" is complex and goes beyond titles. No one even questioned the legitimacy of using the title "Doc'toor" to address a young "moeid" without a Ph.D.

When Egypt became a Republic, President Gamal Abdel Nasser banned titles all together. Society had to get used to addressing men and women as "sayyed/a" or 'ustaz/a', equivalent to Mister and Ms. We were spared the headache of titles at least for a while, although some clung to old titles privately. Praising those who were in power or who were rich continued with various degrees of sophistication, ranging from the vulgar and distasteful to the more refined and subtle. Nowadays, after more than five decades, the use of titles has returned with a vengeance, to the point of utter confusion. The title of "Bashmohandis" (Senior Engineer), once highly valued, is now commonly used to address individuals with minimum education who have no relation whatsoever to engineering. As for the title "Doc'toor" it is frequently used to address thousands who have neither the intention nor the desire to study for the degree. A religious title, "Hag" which literally means: "The one who went on Pilgrimage" (to Mecca for Moslems and to Jerusalem for Coptic Christians) has, likewise, been totally corrupted by misusing it to address individuals who are only remotely religious. Hyperinflation of the use of titles led those in power to use multiple titles at the same time, which is ridiculous as well as comical. A recent former governor of Alexandria was addressed as: Respectable Commander Engineer Almuhafez (Governor) Hassan Beyk! Some address university professors by "Professor Doctoor Ali Beyk". However, one must note that title exaggeration is not a uniquely Egyptian phenomenon. To site one example, Horatio Nelson, who was a British Navy Admiral, had the full title of: Vice Admiral of the White The Right Honorable Horatio, Viscount Nelson, Knight of the Most Honorable Order of the Bath at the time of his death. In addition to this, he had numerous other titles including Baron Nelson of the Nile.

In the era of beautiful days, as Egyptians refer to the Fifties, each tram station had a different architectural style and a unique name such as Zizinia, San Stefano, Rushdi Pasha, Mostafa Pasha, Azareeta and so on. Each stop had a special ambiance, depending on the kind of passengers that came aboard and the district in which the station was located. It was fun to watch pretty women with fancy clothes ride the tram; it was a sort of perpetual Parisian fashion show as they walked elegantly along the "catwalk" separating seats, displaying their beautiful clothes. Women, characterized as the "tender sex", promptly received several seat offers. When an especially attractive woman showed up, a game of sorts started. Admiring men looking and flirting subtly initiated some blushing, acting uninterested followed by occasional quick glances or smiles to keep the game going. This game, perfected by young men and women, involves proper timing and the agility of shifting modes, depending on the response: what I call a fast feedback reaction. Women, who were expected to project a sense of formality and modesty, were more sophisticated in flirting with their eyes and using their facial gestures subtly without being forward, and were more fluent in body language conversation.

For four years, I got on the tram at Gleem station, the name of the district where I lived with my family during the college years. The name Gleem is short for Gleemonopolo who was a rich Greek developer. Waiting for the tram at Gleem station gave me the opportunity to meet friends who lived in the same district. Several college girls lived in a small nearby dormitory, which was basically a villa rented by the University for that purpose. It was fun meeting some of them and exchanging smiles. Sometimes, when I was late, I missed that opportunity, having to run and finally jump on the tram steps in a stylish way, a technique I was happy to finally master.

One day I was not late, and I could afford to walk calmly and slowly, like a prestigious "moeid". Walking along the road that led to the tram station from the Corniche (the seaside boulevard) was socially enjoyable. Frequent greetings accompanied by waving the hand and saying good morning, "sabah elkheir", to the barber, the butcher, the ice cream maker, the grocer, the bike rental shop, the shoe repair man, the newspaper man, several owners of variety shops, and several old porters. They often addressed me 'Ahlan ya Doc'toor", and were proud of me being part of our community.

I could hear the tram coming, so I had to hurry up as it appeared at a distance. I noticed my organic chemistry professor, Dr. Gabrah, who also lived in Gleem, so I greeted him. I liked him, even though he was very formal and stern. When he lectured, his teeth appeared as if he was smiling, which was definitely not true. In fact, students always remembered a poem warning that if the lion's teeth are visible, do not assume that the lion is smiling. I had learned a lot from Dr. Gabrah. My long and well organized lecture notebooks testify to this. He showed us how the structures of complex natural products were elucidated. This involved the performance of several chemical reactions to solve a part of the puzzle. At the time, there were very few of the fancy instrumental techniques available now that help significantly in determining molecular structures without resorting to laborious chemical reactions. Although most of the details are now forgotten, the scientific methodology and logical thinking remain engraved in my memory. My liking of Dr. Gabra, which is in fact a mixture of admiration and respect, also survived the times.

After a few stations, Mostafa Pasha station approached. Mostafa Pasha, was the district where Khaly Labeeb, my maternal uncle (Khaly), lived. I was always delighted to see him. He was jovial, transparent, and fun to talk to. Sure enough, he was taking the tram that day. After saying hello, which involved hugs and kisses, he started talking to me, or, more accurately, appeared to be doing so. He liked to involve nearby passengers in our conversation, so even though he was addressing me, his loud voice and gestures were clearly directed somewhere else! He asked me," So Ashraf, are you going to Amreeka? Are you going to Floreeda?" knowing very well that America and Florida were my destinations. This collateral communication was very amusing, but was sometimes a bit embarrassing.

After a few stops, Khaly had to get off the tram, but I had to continue to "Ramleh Station" down town. One of the ladies listening to our earlier conversation started another one by asking me if I was happy to go to America, which I answered affirmatively. Luckily the chat was short as she left the tram at the following stop. Even though such conversations are entertaining, I cherished moments when I could review events, fantasize and evaluate.

The Fellowship

Finally, I was left alone the rest of the ride, and I gazed through the window, recalling the momentous event when I read my name in the newspaper as one of three students selected for one of the fellowships to study for a Ph.D. at Florida State University. I was simply ecstatic to the extent that I felt my hair stand up for the first and only time in my life, so far.

Before, I had regularly dreamt of going to America to study even though the likelihood was small because study missions abroad were suspended for budgetary reasons. I kept bragging that I would go to Floreeda (Florida), since I had heard that two fellowships had been offered last year by one professor from Florida State University, which the Ministry of Higher Education accepted and announced as regular government missions. I was told by a top official, "Who knows, perhaps we will get a similar offer again this year!" This remote possibility was my only hope, and strangely enough that was exactly what happened. Two fellowships were offered, one in biochemistry, and another in physical organic chemistry for which I applied. With my name in front of me as one of the three chosen for the biochemistry fellowship, I was overjoyed.

I recalled with great pleasure and self-admiration how a few months ago I had succeeded in my senior year with First Honors in chemistry, a rather big achievement by any standard. Only two others, a Syrian, Abdallah, and a Greek Egyptian, Anastasia, succeeded in doing the same. I recalled how I became one of only four, out of a class of about two hundred, to qualify and earn the opportunity to be in that special small group. It was a kind of an elite group; we had the privilege of having exclusive classes in addition to classes given to all seniors. I said "Bravo" to myself recalling the entertainer who had come to our elementary school several years before. Every time he was about to perform one of his "remarkable" acts, such as whirling while carrying heavy weights on his shoulders or putting fire or blades in his mouth, he asked us to applaud for him saying, "Applause for encouragement." It resonates better in my ears in Arabic, "Taseefaa Lil tashgeea". That is exactly what I was doing for myself!

Tens of young, distinguished chemistry graduates competed nationally for these two very rare fellowships. I was the youngest and highly qualified, but one could never be sure. Rereading my name in the paper to reassure myself that I wasn't in a dream made me relive the intense pleasure I felt when I first saw my name in print. I could not wait to leave the bus I was riding en route to the Faculty of Science to tell my friends in college, and later to my family. Complete satisfaction was delayed because the American professor who offered the fellowship stipulated that he would make the final choice from the three selected by the Egyptian Ministry of Higher Education. I somehow felt that luck was on my side. After all, didn't I learn regarding the fellowships the very last day before the expiration of the deadline from my relative who coincidentally read the announcement and told me? Weeks passed as I waited for the final choice of the American professor. As time dragged on, the excitement subsided, but suddenly surged upon the arrival of a letter from Florida State University. One could imagine the level of excitement trying to open the letter, I was selected for the biochemistry fellowship, but the starting date was set for the following fall. Well, I was thrilled that I was chosen and that I would be going to Amreeka. There were a couple of flies in the ointment however. I would be leaving later than expected. I was hoping that I would be chosen for the Physical Organic fellowship, which I thought was closer to my chosen field of Physical Chemistry. Instead, I was selected for the Biochemistry fellowship. I thought that somehow I would deal with that matter when I arrive in Tallahassee. I tried hard to convince myself that Biochemistry would be all right -pardon me, I should say "OK". My heart, though, remained with Physical Chemistry that deals with theories that govern chemical processes and phenomena arising from the interaction of matter, magnetic and electric fields and structural information derived from such observations. Anyhow, there were five long months before my departure, and many things could happen, so it was better, I told myself, to postpone excessive anticipation and excitement until departure time approaches. I used this mechanism often, to protect myself, at least partly from big disappointment.

The tram finally arrived at its final stop. I stepped down and started walking towards my college which was in "Moharrum Bey", a popular district of Alexandria. The college is on a mound and one has to climb steep steps to reach it. The Faculty of Science buildings were formerly a large High School with gardens, a soccer field and a large hall for serving meals. A fancy beautiful house used by headmasters now houses the Mathematics Department. The collection of buildings used to house newly established Farouk University. Later, all colleges except the Faculty of Science were transferred to other sites. The name of the University was changed to Alexandria University after the military coup/revolution in 1952 at the end of my second college year.

As I walked, I thought of another damper of my pleasure. I was hoping that my friend, Hanna, an Alexandrian Coptic Christian, who was my laboratory instructor in Physical Chemistry during my fourth year would be chosen for one of the fellowships. He was a polite, jovial fellow, closer to my age and personality than Abdo, the person chosen who would be my companion. Abdo had been my instructor in the first year laboratory. I did not particularly like him, not because of the age difference (he was eight years older than myself), but because I did not appreciate his attitude. Once, I saw him throw the laboratory notebook of a fellow student from the window because he did not like the notes of the student. I thought then, and more so now, that such vulgar behavior has nothing to do with education. Ironically, he later became the chairman of the Department of Chemistry at Alexandria University. I do not believe his attitude changed, but had become better camouflaged. Of course, I was biased towards my friend who loved music and was more refined. We laughed often together.

In contrast, my companion Abdo was not interesting, a bit crude, and not straightforward. The fact that we shared the same religion, Islam, did not make any difference. Like it or not, Abdo was then my companion and I had to learn to interact with him in a friendly manner, and explore positive traits that he must have.

Living in Alexandria

I rewarded myself for my great achievement by living frivolously the first summer after my graduation. I had no more academic obligations or worries about studying. I entered a new phase in my life, even though temporarily, a carefree phase. Gleem where I lived with my family was a fancy neighborhood near one of the most beautiful beaches of Alexandria. In the summer it became crowded with vacationers, mainly from Cairo. In the evening, traffic jammed the street leading to the beach as people flocked to have the famous Gleem ice cream. Till this day, I have not had a tastier, more delicious ice cream anywhere. People were served in their cars, elegant parfait glass cups, containing rich and fresh flavors of chewy ice cream, particularly mango, strawberry, chocolate, and vanilla. The vanilla flavor, "laban" as we call it, was the most popular. Its unique taste comes from "misteka" (gum Arabic).

I spent quite a bit of time swimming at Gleem beach. There was a large rock, a bit far from the beach, which we called "the island", and it was a challenge to reach it by swimming. I was not a good swimmer, but I felt more adventurous, and indeed I met the challenge successfully that summer. It was interesting what heightened self confidence can do to you. I even attempted to compete to reach it faster than my experienced beach companions. How delightful were those moments spent sitting under colorful large beach umbrellas listening to gossip, matching girls and boys, wondering about people in neighboring umbrellas, and venturing to talk to them, eventually. The agony of anticipating food after a long swim was soon rewarded when one of our servants brought home-cooked food, which we consumed in a flash. Often though, we would simply go to one of the nearby sandwich stores, where we would order one sandwich after another. "Please, roast beef", and before finishing it "Please, liver" and later "Please, tongue" "Please, fried brain" until satisfaction was finally achieved. Those sandwiches were tiny, eaten while standing, with hot mustard and an occasional spicy pickle from the accompanying plate. When we were short on money, we would go to a falafel and fool (beans) specialty shop, and anxiously wait for our turn to order. Waiting was tormenting, with abundant appetizing smells, and scenes of others consuming delicious sandwiches. We would watch the cook take a scoop of the bean paste, mixed with fresh vegetables which gave it a distinct light green color with an appetizing smell, and throw it in a large skillet of boiling oil. We watched it sizzle and quickly turn into a light brown color. Watching the cook was itself delightful. His rhythmic repetitive motions producing dozens of falafels with lightning speed was almost hypnotizing. Another person with comparable efficiency took three or four of these cooked falafels and stuffed them in small round pita bread. He would add some sesame paste, fresh tomatoes, some spices, and arugula. Falafel sandwiches were produced one after another. Finally, each of these delicious sandwiches disappeared, as they were gulped with great joy, in anticipation of the next one. Sometimes, our sweet tooth needed satisfaction, so we would go to a "fiteer" shop. Fiteer is a particularly delicious dessert prepared on demand, by rolling the dough, spreading it thin, throwing it repeatedly up in the air, and finally stuffing it with nuts, before folding it neatly and putting it in the oven. Sugar syrup or honey is added, and a fantastic desert is ready to melt in our mouth.

Walking on the Corniche (the seaside boulevard) in the evening or at night after a long afternoon nap was yet another ritual in our frivolous summer days. While walking we ate roasted corn, peanuts, alfalfa sprouts, spicy germinated beans, and roasted seeds called lib which are eaten like sunflower seeds. The perpetual act of opening the lib seeds produced a sound similar to the pronunciation of the Arabic word "azaz". One of my friends was able to have a mouthful of lib, and could perpetually spit out the shells, while eating the seeds, a sort of an automated lib eater. All this was done while watching a parade of young women, and exchanging various messages. Some of my friends were fond of singing western songs that were popular at the time, like " Kiss Of Fire", "Dance With Me" and "A Ma Romeo" the latter was sung by the beautiful Rita Hayworth in that great film, Gilda. I enjoyed listening, and even ventured to sing it myself. We were indeed at the top of the world.

The city of Alexandria at that time had a cosmopolitan atmosphere with large Greek and smaller Italian and Jewish communities. Before the Second World War there was a sizable Italian community. Many buildings of Alexandria, some still in good shape, were Italian in style. The British put most of the Italians in detention camps, and later deported them. There were several districts which had predominantly Greek inhabitants like "Camp Cesar" and "Ibrahimeya." The language we heard in these areas was mainly Greek, and sometimes French, rarely English. I was often intimidated when I could not communicate in French or Greek at shops or theatres where the attendants did not speak Arabic, or refused to do so. At such moments I felt like a stranger in my own country.

I often frequented these districts to go to movie theatres, particularly Cinema La Gaite. The theatre was not that fancy but had that avant garde ambiance. It was always crowded, showed two films and was inexpensive. There were other theatres downtown which were much fancier and showed recently released films. Each downtown theatre showed films of a particular company. Cinema Metro showed Metro Goldwin Mayer films, Cinema Rialto showed Warner films and the newly built Ameer theatre showed Twentieth Century films. Going to the cinema was exciting. It was like going to the opera now and formal attire was the norm. There were many pleasures associated with going to the cinema in the company of friends: flirting with young women and enjoying delicious sandwiches, refreshing drinks, and fancy ice cream. Downtown theatres were elegant, but nothing topped La Gaite, it somehow had a special flavor. There were two theatres along the Corniche, that were more liberal in showing films with sexy scenes like Rizo Amaro, featuring the Italian sexy actress, Sylvana Mangano. Those were modest but not necessarily less sensual compared with today's films that have abundant nudity and explicit sex. I snuck into these theatres, which were particularly thrilling, especially in the winter when the sea was roaring and the wind carried the moisture of the sea to my face. It was a bit of a naughty thing to do, to go to the Metropolitan theatre by the Corniche, and it represented some contradiction for me, since I belonged to a religious political group.

I loved Alexandria in the winter months when it was cool, but not cold, and the city was not crowded with vacationers. During these months, Alexandria belonged to its inhabitants. The city was always clean. Around midnight when we left the movie theatre, workers were busy washing the streets. If Egypt is the gift of the Nile, then Alexandria is the gift of the sea. The sea has several moods and colors as if it were a huge canvas that was different every day. Some days the sea is so calm and blue, and the sun is shining, and on other days, the sea is dark and the waves are high and are constantly slamming the shore and wetting the Corniche. Together, the sun and the sea displayed all the colors of the visible spectrum and untold combinations that slowly changed. The beauty of Alexandria is not simply physical, for which she had plenty, to the extent we called her the Bride of the Mediterranean. Her beauty is intertwined with its remarkable history that predates even her founder Alexander the Great. The city is famous for its remarkable ancient library that no longer exists physically, but is alive in our subconscious for the great knowledge that it spread for centuries like the city's famous lighthouse that guided ancient vessels. In the Fifties, the city was a major center for art, political activism and intellectual activities. During King Farouk's days, in the summer, the seat of government moved to "Boulkly", a district of Alexandria. This brought a surge of social activities and political gossip. It is like moving the President and all top Government officials from Washington to San Francisco for the summer months. My college years in Alexandria were rich, lots of fun and pleasant memory flashes of those days bring instants of happiness until now.

The Family

While I enjoyed living with my family during my college years, the urge to be on my own progressively became stronger especially after graduation. My grandfather "Giddi" combined brilliance with knowledge, wisdom with wit, love of life with an acute awareness of its complexities. From as far as I can remember, he and I developed, what is called in biology, a symbiotic relationship. My grandparents had an apartment building in the Sakakeeny district in Cairo where Egyptians with different religions Moslems, Christians and Jews lived quite amiably. My grandparents' friends and acquaintances reflected this mix of religions. The building was damaged, but remained intact, by a bomb during German and Italian raids targeting British soldiers who were all over Cairo, particularly in Heliopolis, in east Cairo as well as west of Cairo all along the route leading to the large oasis of Fayoum. My grandparents were scared of the bombings, and decided to move in with us, which was exciting news for me. At the time, we were living in Sohaag 400 kilometers south of Cairo. There I attended a nice kindergarten that overlooked the Nile. After nearly seventy years, I remember the school vividly, many teachers, the headmistress and Zebaida, my first love, with her soft dark hair. After my grandparents sold their apartment building in Cairo, they lived with us continuously as we moved from one city to another. That move affected my life in a fundamental way, allowing me to quickly develop a special relation that gave me joy, strength, and wisdom. My memories of "Giddi" still enrich me to this day.

My father was the head of the Land Survey Department, a prominent post with great responsibilities, for it had to do with the most precious property in Egypt: agricultural land. Preparing professional maps for various purposes, including military maps, was part of his job. He was transferred to various Governorates, so every four years or so we moved. After Sohaag in the south we moved to Fayoum, west of Cairo, then to Tanta in the middle of the Nile delta, and then to Alexandria.

My father was not very political. His job and extended family were top priorities. He was an Egyptian nationalist who was against the British occupation and the corruption of the King. He aspired for a society of social justice and adherence to moral values. He joined the Muslim Brotherhood to fulfill this vision but was not intimately involved in political maneuvering or advocacy. He was not an activist like his older brother, Ezzat, who, as a student, participated in massive demonstrations against the British. Ezzat El-Bayoumi was, according to documented history, the first of several hundred Egyptians killed at the onset of the 1919 Revolution.

My father was a highly principled man who valued honesty, and was very strict about protecting public funds. When he was the Head of the Survey Department of the Governorate of Alexandria, I often visited him in his huge, fancy office, which was close to my college in Moharrum Bey. During one visit, an important government official who was in his office addressed me. He said, "Hey, young man, I hear that you are good in drawing faces." Then he grabbed a piece of paper from the top of my father's desk, and asked me to draw his face. "I am sorry," I said. "My father taught me never to use official paper for private use." I respected my father's adherence to principles both publicly and privately. I do not believe the official appreciated my remarks, even though he acted as if he admired my stand, but my father genuinely did. My action was spontaneous and derived from my belief that sticking to principles is not only the correct thing to do, but that approach leads to success. The latter proved to be a very naive expectation. In fact, that trait leads to many losses, material and otherwise. I believe that those who are dedicated to upholding principles must realize from the start that a heavy price will be paid, and have to define success accordingly. I was occasionally admired for this habit, but I was often disliked for it because it made many feel uncomfortable, since it was at odds with their individual interests.

Although my life in Egypt was not only comfortable but also enjoyable, my desire to go abroad was very strong. One important reason was my longing to be free and independent. It is probably the same feeling teenagers have when they finish high school in the US, as I have learnt from my grandchildren. During the four years of college, I lived with my parents, my three brothers and my sister, as most Egyptian students did and still do. Even though I benefited from the conveniences of comfortable living, I, nevertheless, envied those few students who came from small towns or villages and had to live alone in Alexandria. I was anxious to be alone and independent, although such desire was tempered by some fear and apprehension. My family, particularly my mother, was very protective and restricted my freedom of movement and action, even beyond those imposed by financial, societal, and geographical factors. I strongly felt that it was time to take the first plunge into independence and freedom, but little did I know at that time, that I was also embarking on a step that would deprive me from the very independence and freedom that I was seeking. I was taking serious steps towards engagement and marriage!

At the time of my selection for a mission to Floreeda, my father was in political detention in Cairo, and we could not see him. The Free Officer's Movement, FOM, toppled King Farouk's Regime in a bloodless coup and forced his abdication of the throne and replaced him with General Naguib. Nearly all Egyptians were elated by these developments. Hopes for independence from the British and improved living conditions were at an all time high. In fact, I have never seen Egyptians more happy and hopeful as during this period. The new rulers began delivering on their promises of greater social equality and improving living conditions for millions. Early on, rental reductions and agrarian reform, which resulted in distribution of land to poor peasants, had begun. Big land owners who lost most of their huge holdings were angry, and some resisted without success. A young officer, Gamal Abdel Nasser, the actual leader of the FOM, became the President of the new Republic of Egypt.

Initially, the Muslim Brotherhood, MB, supported the FOM which banned all political parties but with the pretext of not being a political party kept the MB legal. Later however, a power struggle began when the MB opposed agrarian reform plans, sided with big land owners and demanded essentially what amounts to a veto power over major decisions. That was a grave mistake which reflected the MB's inflated sense of power. When Nasser was subjected to an assassination attempt in Alexandria, the MB was blamed for it, leading to the mass arrest of its leaders and thousand of its members, among them was my father. Nasser was entrenched in power and became the sole leader of the new Republic of Egypt.

Love In Gleem

During the last few months of my senior year I began to notice the daughter of our neighbors who owned the two story villa in which both our families lived. We rented the lower level with its small garden. It was delightfully surprising to see her suddenly bloom into a young woman. She was still in high school. She went to a private all girls' school, "Sacred Heart", which was run by Catholic nuns. With few exceptions most of the teachers at this school were Irish. The chemistry teacher for upper level students was one of my former professors. He had been dismissed from the University because he allegedly belonged to the Communist party. When he taught, one of the nuns had to attend the class. This chaperoned supervision was particularly amusing to those of us who were used to public schools where male teachers teaching all girl classes was by no means unfamiliar.

When I graduated and secured the position of "moeid", I began for the first time in my life to think about and explore long-term relations with young women. Meeting girls was not easy. There was no dating, no parties, and only occasional encounters in the tram, street, beaches, or movies. Attending the same college gave a rare opportunity to meet a girl and talk with her under legitimate pretexts. In fact, several girls became nervous during their senior years, for that was the last opportunity to get married from the available pool. There were a number of female science students, but I was not particularly interested in any of them. Some of them were Greeks who followed a different set of rules, far more liberal than other Egyptians, both Moslems and Coptic Christians. Greek girls and boys were allowed to meet outside the university, go to movies, and go to Greek clubs. I felt that the presence of Greek students in our college was nice, it added a special touch to college life.

My neighbor, Soo Soo (short for Soheir), quickly became an obsession. Every time I saw her, my heart pounded so fast as if I had run ten kilometers. I asked myself, "Is this love?" Her beauty and demeanor attracted me very much. I also knew that she did very well in school, and was quite bright. What more could I ask for? Unfortunately, there were few opportunities to talk to her directly. She had a friend, Laurette, who was her constant companion and together they spoke French perpetually. I saw her mother from time to time, as she was my mother's friend. On these occasions I made all kinds of excuses to be present. I guess I was trying to impress her, and apparently I was successful. She was both elegant and beautiful, with close resemblance to her daughter. On rare occasions, when Soo Soo was talking to my younger brother, who befriended her and her brother, I would attempt to engage her in some conversation. I was convinced then that I was not handsome, and that my attractive feature was my charisma, displayed when I spoke.

I became increasingly fond of Soo Soo, and when I realized that I was surely going to Amreeka, time became critical. Since time was short and I wanted us to know each other better before leaving, I began to think seriously of formal engagement, the only permissible way of seeing her regularly and knowing her well. I began to put out feelers, sort of trial balloons for my potential acceptability. Since I would soon go abroad, this meant that she had to finish high school in Egypt in two years, and be accepted at Florida State University. I felt I had important assets, being a moeid and going to the States on a study fellowship. At that time, education was regarded as higher than financial standing by the middle class.

My family began to know that I was in the process of selecting a bride. The fact that my father was in political detention dampened any expected excitement about the idea, but acceptability slowly evolved since I would be away for six years or even longer. Apprehension of the possibility that there would be no engagement before my departure would increase the possibility of marrying a foreigner. This helped to support the idea of an immediate engagement before departure. My family members were curious to know if I had someone specifically in mind. I did not give any hint - at least that was what I thought. They began to make one suggestion after another, mostly from extended family members. Some were first cousins, which I dismissed quickly and unequivocally. I had witnessed the added social complications from inter-family marriages. Having studied biology for three years, I was also aware of unnecessary genetic complications. There were no legal or social barriers to marrying first cousins, but I also felt that such marriages are like social short circuits, dangerous and also boring. Exploring possibilities was useful, however. It allowed further assessment of my real choice, and also helped to camouflage my intention until I was ready to announce it.

In the meantime, my love in Gleem grew steadily until I became certain of my choice, and convinced that Soo Soo's mother, a powerful ally in my quest, approved whole heartily. As for approval by her father, this was difficult and for a good reason. Soo Soo was young for marriage and was still in high school. Also there were several similar situations that lead to the breaking of the young woman's heart when her fiancée ended the engagement unilaterally during his sojourn in a Western country. In those situations, the new atmosphere in which young men found themselves, the entirely different courting relationships, as well as the fascination with Western culture, along with complex identity issues were the main causes. In spite of anticipated difficulties, I started the process for the engagement. I asked my grandfather, who was my friend and confidant, if he could guess who I chose to marry. He answered with a smile," Amin's daughter." Engineer Amin was Soo Soo's father. I was surprised at how perceptive my grandfather was. I was happy that he approved, and was willing to have him represent me in asking Mr. Amin for the hand of his daughter in marriage. Meetings for such a request are usually marked by apprehension, and this particular one was no exception. No definite answer was given or expected by me. I would not go through with the idea without Soo Soo's approval. The meeting ended with an expression of some reluctance, but with a promise of serious consideration. Bahareyya, Soo Soo's mother, played a key role in paving the way for approval. This turned out to be ironic a few years later, when she became a determined antagonist after visiting us in Amreeka and disapproving of our living conditions and life style.

A date was set for the engagement party, and, more importantly, I became a frequent visitor of Soo Soo. I had occasions to go out with her, always with a chaperone, but we were left alone for long hours when I visited at her home. I was surprised at the obvious gap between public and private rules. In this instance, the private flexibility made sense. In any case, I greatly appreciated it. I felt that there was a narrow window of time where Soo Soo and I could know each other, and probe our feelings towards each other. Since Soo Soo was six years younger than I, thoughts about love and marriage were suddenly thrust upon her. Quickly, however, we became enchanted with each other. Our love at that stage was romantic, but not purely so. My visits were dominated by conversations, but quickly turned into sessions of inexhaustible, enjoyable kissing. Since kissing and hugging were the upper limit of our physical love, this became an opportunity to perfect that art.

The engagement party was very nice. This is the occasion to exchange gold rings, and I gave Soo Soo a beautiful diamond ring that I bought with the help of my mother, since I was totally ignorant about buying. Besides, my mother knew the family jeweler and had mastered the technique of bargaining. The party went well, though the absence of my father put a cloud and limited our joy. On such occasions, side conflicts often occur as if they are part of the ritual of coupling two families. Our party was no exception, but luckily they were minor and generally restricted to gossip. There was lots of food and delicious desserts. Food is always a nice way of demonstrating hospitality. For me, the party was a necessary formality, although my real joy was being alone kissing Soo Soo and occasionally dreaming of the future.

Time was passing both quickly and slowly. I wanted to spend more time with my fiancé, but I also wanted to leave immediately, for I was worried that I too would be politically detained. Even though I whole-heartedly welcomed the removal of King Farouk, I was hoping for a quick establishment of some form of democracy that allows wider public participation. In my mind I was debating and evaluating political developments and I did not support Nasser at that stage, and my support for the Muslim Brotherhood was declining very fast. Previous gestures by its leader to appease the King, and realization that their interest in achieving power was paramount, were among the major factors leading to this decline. My idealistic expectations were shattered by what I considered opportunistic positions on the part of the leadership. I felt that reevaluation was needed.

The time of departure was set, and Abdo and I would travel by boat to Amreeka at the expense of the Egyptian Government. A friend of the family was courageous enough to arrange for me to visit my father at the military camp where he was detained in Cairo. The whole visit, a very rare event, was shrouded in secrecy. I eventually saw my father. It was nice seeing him and updating him about the family and me, but the visit was far from pleasant. I was used to seeing my father in a position of power, and now a young soldier was ordering him around. The humiliation associated with the whole ordeal left me with bitter and angry feelings at the injustice of it all. I was also very proud of my father for sticking to his principles; particularly that he had the option of avoiding arrest all together if he would compromise those principles. Before his arrest, friends close to the regime gave him that opportunity if he were willing to withdraw his support of the leadership of the Moslem Brotherhood. He refused. Even though his support was declining at that time, he did not think that withdrawing support under those circumstances would be the honorable thing to do. Others who withdrew support were indeed spared arrests, some were rewarded, but all lost respect from people who value principles and honor.

"Bokrah Essafar Bokrah" Travel is Tomorrow

The last few days before departing for the USA were hectic, but enjoyable. I was all set. I had my first Egyptian passport. I selected the chemistry books that I would take and a small sized Quran, our Moslem holy book, to keep in my pocket for protection. I wondered at that time why individuals who carried the Quran with them were not spared misfortunes and even accidental death. If the Quran is meant to be a moral guide for Moslems in their behavior and actions, is it proper to treat it as a relic for protection against envy, accidents and disease, like a "hijab"? These questions puzzled me at the time, but I still felt comfortable carrying the Quran in my pocket just in case! Others, particularly women put gold or silver necklaces that have specific verses of the Quran while several women put a golden lock of various sizes that encloses a small Quran. I will not forget an experience I had many years ago. I was riding a bus taking me from downtown Cairo to Heliopolis, and was standing between two large seats. It was crowded, so I had to lean towards the seated passengers in front of me. Looking directly downwards a fantastic scene greeted me. The vertical angle of my sight allowed me to see a woman's bare, beautiful breasts with a golden pendant case containing the Quran hanging from a necklace right in the middle. When the bus moved, the breasts started to vibrate violently like hard set Jell-O. The woman acted as if nothing was happening, but I got the strong feeling that she was aware and pleased by the dynamic view she was offering. What was remarkable is the striking contradiction represented by the scene of the Quran jumping all over between the jiggling breasts. Modesty of women is strongly advocated by the Quran. There was a man sitting beside her, her husband I assumed. His serious and stern look was amplified by an impressive huge mustache. I kept shifting my sight from the face of the man to the restless breasts, several moments. The contradiction presented by the scene was matched by another, my own. I was enjoying the breast scene even though I should not on the grounds of piety.

"Bokrah Elsafar Bokrah", travel is tomorrow and time to say goodbye. This was not an ordinary goodbye, for it was assumed that I would be away for six or even seven years. At the time, travel back and forth from Egypt to America was a rarity. The only consolation would be correspondence and occasional telephone calls. Even the latter was not that simple: one had to arrange with the operators for availability at both ends. My grandfather, with tears in his eyes, told me, "Who knows Ashraf, if I will ever see you again." I answered, "Of course, I will see you," but in my heart, I thought that the possibility that I may not see him was real. That made me terribly sad. During the last few days my contradictory feelings were tormenting and exhausting me. I had to leave my bed in a hurry to stop dwelling on sad thoughts. Also, that day was the last time I would go to the Faculty of Science to say farewell to my dear friends and professors.

I enjoyed going to my faculty immensely. I spent hundreds of hours in its buildings listening to lectures trying to catch every word and put it in my notes, doing numerous chemical experiments, even being burnt once by boiling sulfuric acid, dissecting frogs and cockroaches, identifying hundreds of insects in the entomology class, and drawing the beautiful complex anatomy figures that Dr. Shukrallah elegantly drew on the blackboard using a multitude of colored chalk. I remembered student election days and political activities, particularly during my second year, when some university students volunteered to fight the British occupation forces that were based in barracks along the Suez Canal. A couple of years earlier, they had their camps in the heart of Cairo and Alexandria, and sometimes emerged from them to violently suppress massive demonstrations that included high school and university students, and occasionally workers. I vividly recalled the big Cairo fire of January 1952, when several hotels and buildings burned. Apparently King Farouk, as well as British intelligence, were behind it in order to provide a pretext for removal of the majority Wafd government, a liberal Nationalist party, and to declare martial law. I was reminded of the Quo Vadis movie scenes showing Rome burning while Nero was presumably playing his lute. I wondered then if the perpetrators in Cairo were also playing music. I remembered the last few months of my senior year when we had a sit-in demonstration in support of democracy and General Naguib. This particular activity delayed and almost jeopardized my appointment as a "moeid".

Going to college as a "moeid" was even greater fun. However, in the beginning, I was terribly nervous as a teacher. My mouth dried up and my heart was pumping at a high rate, but soon afterwards I enjoyed teaching tremendously and was recognized as a particularly gifted instructor. I liked my students and the majority of them reciprocated that feeling and appreciated my style. I considered teaching an honorable and enjoyable activity and I have never abused my authority. Talking and giving directions to students who were my age or older was an interesting experience. I was lucky that my first teaching assignment was to explain laboratory experiments for premedical students. The proportion of young women was particularly high and generally they came from upper classes. The single criterion for admission was the grades obtained in the National High School Examination, "Altawgeeheyya". Those who had the highest grades were able to enter Medical School or the School of Engineering. Medical students had to spend one premedical year at the Faculty of Science. Teaching gave me the opportunity to get close to many beautiful young women, and to talk with them - chemistry of course.

There were lots of activities at college in those days, in contrast to nowadays where fundamentalist ideology is imposed on the society including universities. Then universities were bustling with activities including evening parties, "haflas". In a hafla, we sat in small groups that mixed girls and boys, students and professors, and some of their spouses. We played word games or displayed hobbies. This was the opportunity to hear a professor sing or act, a student play music, and laugh at students as they imitated professors. Female students and a few women professors did not sing, for that was not considered appropriate. During the day, between classes, sports were the dominant activity. As a moeid I was always invited to play volleyball, basketball or soccer although I was a poor player.

Goodbye to Iskendereya was not only to persons, my colleagues, and my friends, but also to places, activities and the atmosphere that I would not see for seven years. I loved my Faculty immensely and I looked forward to the time when I would return as a professor and contribute to its advancement. In spite of various thoughts, my mind and sometimes my lips shouted "Floreeda here I come!"

EPISODE TWO:

Dream Boat

The big day had finally arrived. Feelings were mixed and contradictory. On the one hand, I wanted to leave yesterday for fear of being arrested. Indeed a few weeks after my departure security police came just to do that. In essence, my education mission to Florida spared me political detention with untold far-reaching consequences. I was involved with the Muslim Brotherhood, which had been banned since they challenged the sole authority of the military rule headed by the popular Nasser. My father, who was a leading member, had been in political detention for several months. On the other hand, I wanted to spend more time with my fiancée in Alexandria. The excitement of being romantically in love was thrilling. There is no substitute for gestures, eye and body expressions that lead to warm hugs and romantic kisses, although having sex, even as defined by Bill Clinton, was strictly unacceptable. These, together with the aura and smell of the body, made my heartbeats race wildly when I saw Soo Soo or even thought of her. I did not want all that to abruptly stop and be replaced by memories of a distant love. That could only be partially substituted by phone calls, which would have to be infrequent due to their high costs, or love letters.

I also very much looked forward to traveling to the States to start my graduate studies and to get a taste of American university life as depicted in films like the one with Van Johnson and Esther Williams. Besides, my curiosity regarding many unknowns, even though mixed with a twinge of fear, was overwhelming. I looked forward to being on my own for the first time in my life and to being fully responsible for myself. The anticipation of the trip, being on the high seas, and visiting interesting ports of the Mediterranean was very exciting. Our ship would head eastward towards Beirut in Lebanon, then head westward to Patras in Greece, Naples, Genoa and Livorno, all in Italy, Marseilles in France and, finally, we would reach New York after four weeks.

All bags were packed and finally the time of goodbyes came. I was never fond of such moments, for they are confusing. One has to express varying feelings at almost the same moment, and do it under the probing eyes of many. Saying goodbye to my grandfather was especially sad. We both realized that the possibility of not seeing each other was real. Besides, this was one of the rare times I saw him crying, actually sobbing. Moments like that reveal the depth of a relationship which lead the anticipation of separation to intensify. Of course the opposite is very true also. This now reminds me of a moving scene from a wonderful movie "Cinema Paradiso". Alfredo, the blind affectionate movie projectionist, was saying goodbye to Toto (Salvatore) his dear young friend, cum grand son, who was departing the Sicilian town. As he urged Toto to go and never come back, tears were running over his cheeks. Later, Toto returned to attend the funeral of his loving companion. My thoughts then were quizzing the future to know whether I would see that dear, loving, bright, jovial, blind man I called Giddy, short for Grandfather, who was my mentor, companion, and educator. Flashes of our relationship sparked in my mind while I was giving him my last hug. One short 'film clip' was the sounds of his squeaking, shiny shoes as he walked with his cane on his right hand, and his left hand in my arm. Another memory flash was when he stayed with me very late at night, giving me moral support while I studied for crucial exams.

My dear mother, my brothers, and my kind, loving sister all hugged me; my absent father was more present than any of them, for I had the greatest respect for this principled man. Hugging Soo Soo was a different feeling altogether, certainly unlike hugging her father and mother or members of my family, but also very different from our private hugs. Soo Soo's crying made me realize how quickly our affectionate relationship had developed, as if we had always known each other. I hugged every family member, every servant, every acquaintance and even people I did not know. No wonder the entire commotion made me develop a terrific headache.

Finally, I was alone on the deck of the boat, all alone waving to everyone who was shouting goodbyes and persistent requests of writing regularly. My throbbing agonizing headache continued. Ironically, I was relieved when the boat finally started moving. The boat's typical whistle announced the start of its routine long trip and my much longer trip. After a while, my family became barely visible and finally all members of my entire family merged into a dot in the horizon. Before retiring to my cabin and succumbing to my headache, I stayed a while longer on deck, and watched the beautiful Alexandria skyline fade away and eventually my entire lovely Alexandria became another vanishing dot. It disappeared optically for several years, but remained mentally visible every day. I wanted desperately to rest, and postponed for later the pleasures of delightful expectations and ruminations on what had suddenly become memories. An important ingredient for happiness is the accumulation and then the availability of a pool of enjoyable memories to draw upon as desired, like the camel and its hump.

I went to the cabin I shared with Abdo, who would be my companion on the trip and for several years in Floreeda. The cabin was in the second class of Cleopatra, the cargo-passenger ship we boarded. In spite of the name, it was far from being fancy. Certainly it had no relation to the luxurious cabin where Cleopatra and Antonio enjoyed their love, and my companion was no Cleopatra either. Anyway, one should not be too demanding. Our government, which had a hard currency shortage, paid for the trip after all! That also explains the fact that each one of us was permitted only forty dollars to cover any additional costs until our arrival in Washington, D.C., where we would receive one month's salary, and additional allowances from the Egyptian Education Bureau.

After a much-needed nap, I went to the dining room for my first lunch. I was very hungry, and I was curious as to the quality of the food. I thought also that it would be a good occasion to review and meet the few other passengers on board. The food was good, or perhaps I was very hungry; more importantly it was kind of a novelty for me to eat outside home. As my hunger was being satisfied, I noticed one particular passenger. He was a rather handsome young man who took special attention to cover his mouth while meticulously using a toothpick. His attempt to camouflage his picking act clearly attracted attention. Perhaps the idea was to show others how well-bred he was, particularly to a young woman accompanying her mother. Everything, including people, was strange to me. After a few days on the boat, a routine was established and familiarity gradually replaced novelty. For a few, familiarity developed into intimacy either conversationally or in some cases sexually. My only option was to converse with men or families. I was emotionally occupied with my love to my fiancée and my experience in sex was limited to the newly discovered delights of our passionate romantic kissing.

There were two university professors, both from the Faculty of Engineering at Alexandria University, with their families. One was a flamboyant, confident and quite intelligent person who received his Ph.D. from the States, from Illinois, as I recall. I immediately liked him, he had a lot of experience and it was quite interesting to listen to his stories and comments. Many years later, he became the Governor of Alexandria and even though I disagreed with his politics, we maintained a friendly interaction mainly at the Alexandria University Faculty Club. The other Professor was perpetually complaining about his whining wife and their continuously crying infant, however he was a kind person and somewhat entertaining. Both professors and the would be professors met regularly to chat and discuss various issues; this made the trip between port stops much less boring. The first officer was a young man who from the first day started flirting with the same young beautiful woman who was being flirted with by the tooth-picking Don Juan. It turned out that she was a bride whose bridegroom would be waiting for her in New York. Nevertheless she freely exchanged flirting with the officer and one did not require much imagination to realize that the flirting developed into a pre-marriage training course or a last chance for forbidden but desired love. Presumably, the bridegroom should be grateful for the added pleasure resulting from the gained experience! I felt kind of sorry for the tooth-picking man, for his contrived behavior did not help. What he really needed to seduce the young woman was the ability to offer a first class cabin and other fringe benefits. For the accompanying mother, who was quite sexy though not particularly beautiful, it seemed that hard sex had been on the captain's log board from the beginning. She and the captain hit it off and after one day she and her daughter were upgraded to first class cabins that were conveniently next to the cabins of the captain and the first officer. Was it my vivid imagination when I heard sexual sounds and passionate cries? Perhaps, but her flushed face and clear expression of satisfaction augmented by the added pleasure derived from her cigarette smoking on deck were certainly not imagined. I could also swear that occasionally I smelled hashish smoke while stewards brought their delicious looking food very different from that served to us at regular meals. So that is why some young men opt to become sea officers.

The sea was quite fascinating to me, since I was only used to the sea as viewed from the shores of Alexandria. I enjoyed all the moods of the sea: angry and violent with high waves and gray skies; serene and calm with sun rays warming its surface; and uncertain and hesitant with clouds forming and dissipating, exhibiting varying combinations of the visible spectrum. But the sea viewed from an ocean liner deep inside was quite different; the deep blue color of the water is utterly beautiful. The occasional interruption of the water's surface with gracefully jumping dolphins was, for me, sheer delight. On the boat I interacted with the sea and was not a mere observer; the rhythmic rocking motion of the boat, coupled with the forward movement, was like a seductive dance. I spent hours gazing into the deep blue water dreaming about my future and imagining exciting scenarios. I knew that the color is an illusion, for the water is not blue, but illusions are sometimes preferable to realities.

Beirut, our first stop was not interesting for we arrived at night and we left before we awoke the following morning, thus there was little we could see. I vaguely remember the city as being small compared to Alexandria or to the now exciting and bustling contemporary Beirut. We then reached Patras in Greece. We got a quick glimpse of the city and recalled how Mohammed

Ali, the founder of modern Egypt in the nineteenth century, put down the insurrection of Greeks against the Ottoman Sultan in his quest to build his own regional empire. The Egyptian troops controlled the entire southern peninsula of Morea (Peloponnisos). Later, however, the entire Egyptian and Turkish fleets were destroyed by British, French and Russian warships. It was fascinating to be in places that were abstract names to be memorized in history classes and to see them materialize in front of your eyes. The notion that I was actually traveling and seeing the world was exciting so it mattered less what in fact I was seeing. The next stop would be Napoli (Naples), the city that invented spaghetti and pizza. I was familiar with spaghetti but pizza was an unknown entity to me. As we approached the large harbor of Napoli, I was conscious of the fact that the city had suffered a great deal during the war and expected to still see some evidence of destruction as a result of the allied bombing. In Naples we stayed overnight and we had the opportunity to visit the ruins of Pompeii, which was quite fascinating. As soon as we disembarked, Italian kids who must have noticed that we were visibly confused and lost met us. They asked us if we wanted girls, as we knew very little Italian or more accurately none, the kids made gestures and asked us in if we wanted to "fuck". I was quite embarrassed and tried hard to avoid their persistence. I was more interested in seeing Pompeii. My companion was seven years older and he probably had some sexual experience but even if he were interested, he had no money to spend on such activities.

Time was short so we took a taxi that drove with frightening speed to Pompeii and finally I had the opportunity to see the consequences of Mount Vesuvius' sudden eruption. I read about that ancient event that occurred in 79 AD and had seen movies about the misfortune of the people of Pompeii. The wet ashes resulting from the sudden eruption preserved most of the city and froze forever some bodies engaged in sexual intercourse in one of the favorite Latin sexual positions, as if they were in a state of eternal climax. Chained gladiators with agony frozen forever on their faces were overwhelmed. The demise of Pompeii had been depicted as an expression of the wrath of God, to make an example for mankind. Religious interpretations of earthquakes and other natural calamities sounded ridiculous to me even then, but I did not argue against them.

At night, we went to a café after a long debate to decide whether we had enough cash to have some refreshment as we hesitantly sat at a table. Soon after, two gorgeous women came and sat with us. I was pleasantly surprised how quickly my sex appeal was effective. My pleasure died quickly when my companion cautioned me quickly in Arabic that these girls were prostitutes and will order drinks that we could not possibly afford. My naivete was revealed and my self-admiration was shattered. I had absolutely no first hand experience in these matters; in fact if I had previously met a prostitute in Egypt, I would not have guessed her profession. However, I knew about the subject since there was intense public debate as to whether the government should continue to legalize prostitution or to ban the practice. It is quite interesting to note that prostitution in Egypt was legal during the war period when thousands of British soldiers and soldiers of other nationalities were stationed in Egypt. I presume this was done to comfort the soldiers while they were fighting heroically to protect Democracy, Freedom, and noble causes! Unlike the Japanese, who forced Korean women to do the comforting, the British did it while protecting the inalienable right of "free choice" for women, while allowing them to earn money for their toil. When I was a kid, I distinctly remember walking with my father in Cairo, when we passed a street named Clot Bey, my father mentioned to me that it is the street where bad girls live. I did not know then the nature of their badness, but I knew enough English to read the signs of "Hello Johnny", "Come in Johnny", "Welcome Johnny". I was then puzzled who was that mysterious Johnny or why there were numerous Johnnys. At the time, we learned about Clot Bey in history class. In the early nineteenth century, he was a prominent physician in Egypt during the reign of Mohammed Ali. The French Dr. Clot established military hospitals and the Egyptian medical school in 1828, which is now called "Kasr Elainy". The heroic efforts of this French doctor to combat cholera and plague epidemics in Egypt earned him the title "Bey" which was most prestigious at the time followed later by the title "General". How ironic history is, the man was honored by naming an important street in Cairo after him, but Clot Bey Street became infamous as the prostitutes' street and no one practically knew who Clot Bey was.

Banning prostitution in Egypt in the late-Forties was considered a great victory for virtue, a sort of a cleansing act. Prostitutes left Clot Bey Street. They did not vanish of course but became formally invisible. Time laundered the tainted image of the street together with the name of Dr. Clot Bey, which gradually lost the connection to prostitutes. Anyway, it was in Napoli that for the first time I came face to face with two beautiful Italian women who were colleagues of former residents of Clot Bey Street.

We passed by a tiny island called Elba off the coast of Tuscany, this was the only Empire Napoleon had since he was exiled after his first forced abdication in 1841. Scenes of his successful escape after only a few months of exile and his successful return to power crossed my mind. He managed to escape in spite of British naval patrols. Among many of the stories I had read about Napoleon, was one about a French reporter who symbolizes to me the epitome of hypocrisy, not a rare characteristic of many contemporary climbers of all sorts. He wrote that the dictator, the butcher Napoleon escaped and landed in southern France. He ridiculed Napoleon's ambitions to rule France again. Every week as Napoleon advanced and his former Republican guard rallied around him the reporter became milder in his attacks. As Napoleon marched in triumph towards the gates of Paris the reporter wrote that thousands were preparing for a huge reception of the "Great Emperor" of France. But to be fair to that correspondent I must add that some officers experienced such sudden change in heart, perhaps prompted by the reaction of ordinary soldiers who adored their champion who on one occasion opened his coat and asked them to kill him if that was their wish. One can imagine the dramatic scene of the wild cheers of the soldiers.

Our ship passed Elba towards Livorno on the Italian coast. We had a few hours to visit Pisa about 25 kilometers away. I looked forward to see the Leaning Tower of Pisa, "La Torre di Pisa". The architects did not intend to build a leaning structure, but the poorly laid foundation and the soft soil we were told, caused the tower to lean to the southwest. We climbed about three hundred steps to the top and were thrilled to see the beautiful surroundings.

As an aspiring scientist, the Tower was where Galileo Galilei dropped two balls of different masses and showed that they had the same speed thus reaching the ground at the same time. Such a story could be just a tale similar to that of Newton's apple, but nevertheless useful. To prevent the collapse of the Tower, the bells were removed and cables were installed in the 1990s and some soil was removed from one side and the Tower returned to its position occupied in 1838. Now it is claimed that the tower is stabilized and has stopped leaning any further. Returning to the ship we continued moving towards Genoa. We stopped very briefly in Genova, or Genoa, as Italians pronounce it.

We passed by Toulon in Southern France, which also sparked historical memories. After all, it was in Toulon where Napoleon's expedition to Egypt started. On May 19, 1798, Napoleon slipped in darkness with his fleet trying to escape the watchful eyes of the British fleet led by the daring Admiral Horatio Nelson aboard the HMS Vanguard. Nelson tried in vain to locate the French fleet and to know its destination. Eventually the two fleets would collide at the famous battle of Abu Qir Bay where Nelson prevailed and the French flagship Orient was sunk, along with the ambitions of Napoleon in Egypt. Another escape by Napoleon landed him in France to pursue his ambitions in Europe. Nelson also continued his military conquests, but on the way he was conquered by Emma, Lady Hamilton, who was a maid, actress and prostitute before marrying Sir Hamilton.

The Nelson-Emma affair was encouraged by her husband and the three lived together for many years. These juicy memories were interrupted by another affair going on our boat when the first officer's room opened and a lady flushed with pleasure lit her cigarette as usual.

Our final stop in the Mediterranean was Marseilles, or Marselia, as we pronounced in Arabic. We landed and had a chance to walk along the sea boulevard similar to the Corniche in Alexandria. I felt hungry and was forced to tap into my forty dollars and had a sandwich in one of the cafés, the most expensive sandwich which I had till then.

Reading a pamphlet about Marseilles I discovered that the chateau made famous in the novel of Alexander Dumas "The Count of Monte Cristo" is near by, although we unfortunately did not have time to visit. I had read the novel when I was in high school, it fascinated me.

Back to the ship, we continued the routine of eating, sleeping, discussions, gossiping, getting irritated with constantly whining children and their quarrelling parents, noticing or imagining love episodes, until we reached Gibraltar at the southernmost tip of Spain. Its name is a modification of the Arabic name "Jabal Tarek" which means the mountain of Tarek. Tarek was the Moslem commander who invaded Spain in the early eighth century. The Moslems ruled most of Spain for several centuries. Geographically Gibraltar or the "Rock" is part of Spain, however it was ceded to the United Kingdom in the early eighteenth century, and it became strategically important for the British Navy as it controls the passage between the Mediterranean and the UK as well as the Atlantic Ocean. It had been a significant crossing point between Africa and Europe since the dawn of humanity. So Gibraltar figured highly in both contemporary and early history, and remains a point of contention between Spain and the UK. It was a fascinating moment passing through the Straits of Gibraltar.

Now we were on the last and longest leg of the trip. In spite of occasional boredom, the ocean voyage gave me time to reminisce, to clear my thoughts and even to review my knowledge of chemistry. After all I was not on a vacation even though it felt like it. The reality was that I was starting a long trip of learning and research at FSU. I was also carrying a whole load of culture, rules, contradictions and thoughts, some in a premature state of development, some on their way for rejection and some that I would adhere to. The wide ocean was very helpful in allowing me to sort out and perhaps redefine all of that and think boldly about my true values. I was always confident and above all, looking forward and excited to go to the great Emerald City, the Wonderland, the U.S.A.

EPISODE THREE:

On Broadway

Finally, we arrived at our destination on a sizzling hot day in August 1955. The hassle of collecting my old style leather suitcases and going through customs and immigration at New York Seaport was quite consuming and it robbed me from the excitement of reaching Amreeka the Wonderland. I was helped greatly by our companion who had studied in the States and was familiar with the terrain. I was also severely strained by the limited dollars in my pocket, which compelled me to under tip and be unusually stingy. A group of us went to a reasonably priced hotel in Manhattan. We rested and did minimal unpacking as we planned to leave New York after one day. Time passed quickly and it was night. In spite of being tired, I could not resist the temptation of going out with few of my companions to walk in the heart of Manhattan.

It is hard to recall the extent of my excitement walking in the famous streets of Manhattan. The experience was nothing short of being psychedelic. Several years later, I heard the same description given by an American scientist for his first days in Cairo. All the senses are stimulated by unfamiliar signals. Unfamiliar sounds, scenes, smells as well as tastes were amplified by wild expectations and imagination creating an amalgam of shear fascination. I saw ahead of me what appeared to be a flying train going across in the sky. Wow! A few seconds later, I realized that it was one of those ticker advertisements. The smoking guy perpetually puffed a Lucky Strike or Pall Mall. This was in the mid-Fifties long before the famous Marlboro Cowboy. Glittering light was all over flashing from movie theatres, shops with loads of clothing and gadgets. Crowds from different countries were gazing at window shops, sounds of different languages interfered to constitute a hybrid language that defied comprehension.

In the morning our group dispersed, some went to Washington D.C., others to Illinois. Abdo and I planned to stay one more night to have a chance to see more of New York or, more accurately, more of Manhattan. I only hoped to see a few landmarks but Radio City Music Hall was on the top of the list. Going down to the lobby of the hotel, I had my first glance at a television screen. Television came to Egypt shortly after I left. Such moments are quite memorable - the first time to hear and acquire a radio, the first time to fly, witnessing the first man orbiting the Earth or walking on the moon or the first time to use a computer. My children, and particularly my grandchildren, take these gadgets as if they were created shortly after the Big Bang. I wonder what exciting first moments my grandchildren will witness in the future! "So this is television", I exclaimed. The show being watched casually was Tic-Tac-Toe or something like it. The show itself was certainly not remarkable but the medium carrying it definitely was. It was surprising that individuals who were competing on the show were winning quite valuable items, more astonishing to me that among the sponsors of the show providing all these items was a company that produces a shoe polish. I wondered how a product like that can bring huge profits. I convinced myself after making some rough calculations that that was indeed possible given the large American market which also justifies the advertisement expenses including the lavish gifts provided to the lucky few. It was not difficult even then to surmise that millions of consumers were the real providers of such gifts for the lucky few.

We walked on streets near our hotel, and our first task was to have breakfast. It was not easy to communicate with our heavy accents and modest vocabulary but we finally managed. New Yorkers must be experts in spotting tourists; it must be the clothes, the wondering eyes and expressions of being lost. Anyway we were spotted by a man in his thirties who offered to show us around. I was suspicious of the man and said so in Arabic to my Egyptian companion. The guy was persistent. We followed him as we had little to fear, did not have any valuables and were in public places anyway. Nevertheless, my discomfort lingered. He took us to see the skyscrapers, Grand Central Station, Penn Station and, of course, Central Park. Those who live in New York are not awed by such places. Similarly, Cairenes who pass by the pyramids frequently lose that fascination with such magnificent structures. It would be nice if our brains kept exciting moments vividly alive in our memories. Few of us can recall such moments with the same intensity felt at the time. Unfortunately, this also applies to the first heart beats of glancing for the first time at a gorgeous attractive woman. They say familiarity breeds contempt, it also dulls sharp excitement.

For me, I could not hold my reaction of amazement when I first saw the Empire State Building. I was not interested in the numbers our companion mentioned- more than one hundred floors, the year it was completed and other details. To me, the sight was more than enough. The ride in the fast elevator that made my heart sink and the view from the top was breathtaking. He also showed us the Chrysler Building. We walked along streets with names such as Wall Street, Fifth Avenue and Forty Second Street, all of which I had first heard about in movies. Our long walk took us to Central Park. It was pleasant seeing many bikers, people of all ages strolling and riding horse carriages. Our volunteer guide who apparently knew the history and the geography of New York well told us that Manhattan is an island that lies at the end of a river called the Hudson and it derived its name from a Native American "Red Indian" word which means island of many hills. After an enjoyable but trying tour, we thanked our American companion who certainly was generous with his time. It was rewarding to follow him. Suspicion coupled with open-mindedness proved useful. This is similar to the phrase coined by President Reagan in relation to Soviet disarmament: "Trust but Verify", or in Russian "doveryai, no proveryai."

In the evening, we went to Radio City Music Hall and saw a dazzling show of the dancing Rockettes. Such a select group of beautiful women dancing in synchrony while displaying their flawless legs fascinated me. In the morning we had another walk on our own and passed by the United Nation headquarters. The modern building of the UN was impressive, but did not impress me as much as the skyscrapers. We passed by a cafeteria where I was determined to use what my professor at Alexandria urged me to use, "the automaton," as he called it. I put the correct change and made a selection for a sandwich. Sure enough, the correct sandwich came through after a rotation to place it properly. Eating it was anticlimactic as it was not particularly tasty, but I had to be satisfied with the fun of getting it.

Our last stop was Penn Station to get tickets to Washington D.C. Arriving in the capital of Amreeka, it was surprising how Washington was more like an average sized town, less crowded and had a large number of African Americans. We had no time to see the sites in DC. Our task was solely to go to the Egyptian Education Bureau to announce our arrival and to get our first check and make sure that our monthly checks that supplemented our fellowship checks would arrive in time at our final destination. I still remember how difficult it was finding the Education Bureau at Decatur Place and how we agonized to find Florida Avenue. I thought then how it was easy to find places in New York City with its parallel streets and perpendicular avenues. D.C., in contrast, did not make any sense to me. Finally, we took the train from the D.C. train station to Jacksonville, Florida where we had to take another train to Tallahassee where more excitement and plenty of surprises awaited me.

EPISODE FOUR:

Colored Water

There I was in the USA after a long boat trip from Alexandria on a train ride racing towards my final destination, Tallahassee. I felt great and at the top of the world, completely independent and nothing standing in my way to fulfill my dream of completing my Ph.D. in chemistry and eventually becoming a scientist. True there were many unknowns, but this in itself made matters more interesting and even exciting, I was never the type who desired a life that is highly predictable or greatly programmed. Picasso once said: "If you know exactly what you are going to do, what is the point of doing it?"

There was one annoying aspect, I really did not want to specialize in Biochemistry, the branch of Chemistry for which I received the Ph.D. fellowship. These matters could wait, I thought then. Somehow things will work out in a desirable manner. I thoroughly enjoyed the prospect of doing research and becoming a scientist. Even then my objective was not receiving a Ph.D. as an end in itself, something I have never doubted would be achieved anyway. My excitement related mainly to the process, the environment, and the joy associated with scientific research. Enjoying the moment and postponing serious issues until the appropriate time allowed me to better focus on these issues and make the hard decisions required. This was a trait that I had then, continued to evolve and proved quite useful to me over the years.

The train had just left the Washington D.C.'s Union Station heading for Jacksonville, Florida. Everything, however trivial, attracted my attention.

People, how they dressed, talked, behaved, and places, including the train station with its huge size, cleanliness, food stands and even the train itself. My focus had always been on comparing what I saw in Amreeka with Egypt, train stations included. I was willing to acknowledge aspects that impressed me, others which alienated me. My Egyptian companion did not express his feelings as outwardly as I did and it was difficult to know how he felt or reacted.

One thing I liked about traveling on a train, and later on a plane, is that I felt a sense of detachment that gave me an ability to look at myself from a distance and gain a sense of clarity. It was as if one was watching a movie of oneself in the past, present and future with an ability to edit events. I could choose to be generous or critical with myself to the degree I desired, depending on the mood. It was a great exercise that permitted me to review various scenarios of future events, a kind of interactive movie, to use contemporary lingo. It was like directing a movie without restrictive rules. I jumped from the past to the future and back to the present instantaneously and with great ease, speaking of the impossibility of time reversal!

Only a few weeks ago, I was in Alexandria, Egypt living with my family constrained in my movements. Next, I was on a train thousands of miles away, completely on my own. This was quite a liberating experience specially when felt for the first time. Obviously I was not totally free, for I carried with me loads of other types of constraints: cultural, religious and social, which proved later to be far more limiting than those imposed by parents.

The important thing was that I was in the USA on a train cutting across southern states, the names of which I heard in American movies before: Georgia, Virginia, South and North Carolina. I had seen several action films dealing with the Civil War, cowboys and "red" indians. Some specific movies came to mind: "Johnny Guitar" with Joanne Woodward, "Broken Arrow" with James Stewart and, of course, the fascinating "Gone with The Wind" with Vivian Leigh and Clark Gable. My thoughts during those early moments in the USA reflected my impressions about America. Those impressions were essentially derived from the movies, which I went to frequently, a bit from the Egyptian media, and some readings including American propaganda booklets distributed during the last phases of the Second World War. Very little knowledge was obtained from first hand experience of Egyptians who visited the USA or who studied there. Most Egyptians at that time went to Europe, particularly Britain to obtain advanced degrees in engineering or various fields of science. Some went to France to study law or literature; others went to Switzerland or Germany to study chemistry. Often third world individuals also studied in countries that colonized them and they came back imitating the colonizer just as the great philosopher/social scientist Ibn Khaldoun described seven centuries ago.

In Egypt, the British model was the one to emulate. This meant a pipe, a British accent which was actually a blend of a British and a heavy local Arabic accent, what we call a twisted tongue, or "lisan maawoog". In addition, a few clearly contrived mannerisms were designed to show that the individual mastered elements of what some perceived as a superior British culture. In advanced cases of such an ailment, the young professor brought from abroad a blue eyed blonde usually of modest beauty and limited education whose previous job was menial such as a waitress or a movie theatre ticket clerk. But who cares, the important thing was that she is blonde and European. The overt self satisfaction and pride by the young professor clearly showed at social gatherings when others reacted with awe and admiration. That was mixed with amusement when the blonde wife uttered one or two Arabic words with her distinguished accent: *"Mish Ma'ooooooool"* meaning innnnnnnnncredible, or "Ahlaan" meaning welcome, or "Alhamdu lillah" meaning thank God. I suspected that was exactly the reaction sought in the first place! Her Egyptian partner does the opposite act as if he forgot some Arabic words and unnecessarily injected a few English words, often with a funny accent that exposed his poor English: "brobaply" (probably) and "sankes" (thanks). Of course, there were practical and opportunistic aspects of such relations. Being married to a British woman enhanced greatly the possibility of being in more prestigious social circles and in some cases closer to the ruling elite or, at least, rubbing shoulders with them. Many such marriages collapsed quickly. There were cases where relationships were more genuine and mature where both members of the couple were comfortable with their individual identities. However, those were the exceptions.

I had the advantage of starting my research in Egypt with a US educated professor, he was the only one in the Department who studied at Colombia University for his Ph.D. and then went to Yale University as a postdoctoral fellow. He was not an easy person to interact with but was a very intelligent man who felt strongly, with some justification, that his talents were not appreciated enough. That made him very frustrated, even bitter. He gave me a condensed summary of his version of life in the USA. A younger professor in geology who spoke with an American accent and displayed American mannerisms such as wearing a bow tie, brightly colored shirts (very unusual at the time), and used terms such as "OK", "see you later", "right you are", "how come?" and "howdy". All were quite novel. He also volunteered some information about Amreeka. I must not forget advice which was given to me by one of my relatives, a senior officer in the Egyptian Air Force: "If you date an American girl, do not expect to mount her the first date. Take your time."

Thus my vision of America was obviously quite limited and was dominated by the notion that every thing is remarkably different from what I am used to- simply a Wonderland. In fact, when I was a high school student I saw a propaganda pamphlet distributed with the same title "America the Wonderland." It sounded more dramatic in Arabic: "Amreeka Balad Elaagayeb". In that booklet I learned that in one national park, probably Yellow Stone Park, one can go fishing at one of the beautiful lakes and after catching the fish turn around and cook it in one of the hot geysers. I read also somewhere that in America cows are lead to one side of a factory and, in few minutes, delicious canned corn beef came out on the other side of the factory. I expected every person in America to have a fancy car: a Cadillac, a Buick or at least a Chevrolet. Vending machines are every where, you just put coins in and, voila, a sandwich, a candy bar or a coca-cola bottle falls into your hand. In short, America is a fantasy land where people have lots of fun, work a little, and are generally naïve. In fact, I thought that graduate school would be a breeze, mainly fun with wild parties like those I saw in the movies. I expected that this would be particularly true in Florida, which I perceived as a sort of playground. After all, Florida was where Esther Williams displayed her swimming talents in those dazzling shows in the famous movie with Van Johnson "Bathing Beauties", or in Arabic "Alsabihaat al Fatinaat".

Beauties would surround me, and surely some of them will be attracted to one of the descendants of Pharaoh Tutankhamun (King Tut). Before departing, I boasted to my friends and relatives in Egypt before departing that I would go frequently to Miami with its fancy beaches and dazzling night shows that we had seen in movies. In fact, it was feared by some that those beauties would soon make me forget my fiance. Senior family members and friends gave me a clear warning not to play around and "play with your tail", the equivalent of the Arabic "ewaa telaab be-dailak". They were seriously concerned that it is only a matter of a few weeks before me sending a letter to my folks telling them that I intend to dissolve my engagement. The lure of the swimming beauties could prove too much and become simply irresistible.

Back to the train ride, we finally arrived at Jacksonville train station. We had to carry our heavy bags to another train that should take us to our final destination, Tallahassee. We each had a couple of hundred dollars freshly received from the Egyptian Education Bureau in Washington and we had to be conservative in spending them not knowing what lied ahead. Using our heavy accented English we finally managed to identify the train and were directed to one particular carriage. We obediently carried our bags and settled in two joining seats and waited for the train to move. I was surprised to notice that the train carriage is not particularly clean. As a matter of fact, it was not well lighted and simply depressing. Mind you, I was interpreting every thing positively. After all, I am in America the Wonderland and every thing ought to be nothing less than fantastic. However, the inescapable truth was that the carriage was dull and dirty. As a matter of fact, second class trains in Egypt were cleaner and fancier. Something was wrong!

When some foreigners come to the USA, they become homesick, perhaps out of nostalgia and feeling alienated and insecure. They feel that everything back home was superb and complain about everything they saw, at least during the first few months in the USA. Other foreigners do exactly the opposite. Everything American is great and they become overly critical of their home countries. In fact, this signals the first step of detachment and changing one's identity. In my case, I strongly identified with Egypt. In fact, part of my dream and a dominant driving force for me was to return to my university at Alexandria after finishing my studies and become a leading scientist there. At the same time, I was utterly fascinated by being in Amreeka. True, I felt a bit intimidated by the fact that my accent in English was not well understood. My vocabulary was not as good as I thought. All that did not matter since I felt confident that after few weeks my English would be perfect and I would communicate fluently and with ease. As we say back home, I would speak "zayy el baraband" or like a chatterbox. Language would not be a barrier for expressing myself or projecting my personality that many believe to be delightful. Some went as far as labeling me as being charismatic. I tended to agree.

I was totally involved in my daydreams when my travel companion suddenly pointed out a fact that should have been quite obvious. All the passengers in our carriage were "Negroes", a term we had picked up from Americans that we had randomly met during the first few days of our arrival. It was strange that I failed to notice. I guess I was totally oblivious of race issues at that time. I looked at the next carriage and sure enough all the passengers were so called "White". We had been placed with the "Negroes". It is difficult to explain my feelings at that moment. I was completely dismayed, disgusted and also insulted. If the "Negroes" are treated with such disrespect, scorn, and contempt to the extent that they have to travel separately in a dirty carriage, then we too were treated likewise. I had great pride, and I thought no one can insult me like that. "Let us move to another carriage," I told Abdo, but he cautioned me that we are in a foreign country and we have to abide by the rules. I would not accept any of that. I was moving to another carriage, alone if necessary. Abdo followed me realizing the extent of my anger and my insistence. Nothing happened, absolutely nothing. We sat with the "Whites". This may have quenched part of my personal indignation but I was disgusted, puzzled and disappointed at the way "Negroes" are treated as if they are less than "Whites". My notion that "Amreeka" is the land of equality where individual dignity is sacred was shattered. I even felt somewhat insecure. My feeling towards "Negroes" was mixed, certainly sympathy but I must admit disgust at them. How can they take this and why don't they refuse such subhuman treatment? One may say that this reflected a high degree of naivete and ignorance about the issue, but that was how I felt. To get a brief taste of humiliation and insult was very instructive even though my immediate reaction was that I am not a "Negro". In Egypt there are definitely class prejudices but they do not reach the level of segregation in trains. However, segregation is of course automatic for the poor who can not afford tickets in the first or second classes in trains or in movie theatres. As students we sometimes traveled in the third class on trains and tramways. It did not bother us in the least. In fact, it was a kind of novelty. Of course, when we had a little extra money we showed off by going first class. The situation with our parents was different. Being middle class they never used third class. So the concept of racial segregation which was thrusted upon me suddenly was totally new. I must say it left me with profound negative feelings at various levels. It is true that I knew of slavery in America and that the slaves were brought forcibly from Africa, but my limited information was that Lincoln freed them long ago after the North won the Civil War. I could not imagine that black people in America were mistreated like that. We in Egypt call blacks "sood". In fact, the name Sudan which is our southern neighbor is derived from this Arabic word. There are blacks in Egypt and they ride the same buses and go to the same schools. There were kids that often joked with them and teased them about their color. Kids also teased those who are short, tall or have large noses simply to annoy them, with limited success sometimes.

It took some time for my feelings of rage and insult to subside, but the issue lingered in the back of my mind. Looking through the train window I noticed that the earth was not black like the fertile soil of Egypt. As a matter of fact, the name of Egypt means the land of black earth. Silt from Ethiopia filled the Nile water for centuries and bestowed fertility on the land. This is why the Ancient Greek historian Herodotus made his old and famous statement:" Egypt is the gift of the Nile", in Arabic: "Masr hebatol neel".

While I was immersed in my thoughts I began to think of the fast approaching final destination: Tallahassee. A disturbing thought haunted me.

Even though Tallahassee is the capital of Florida I had never heard of it before learning that I would be studying there. Capitols are always the biggest cities of a state or of a country aren't they? So Tallahassee must be larger, more glamorous than Miami which is one of Florida's cities and is not even the capital. So my expectations of Tallahassee were high.

Finally, the train stopped at Tallahassee. I was busy carrying the bags and leaving the train but my mind was filled with anticipation. I was expecting an elegant, large and modern station befitting the capital of Florida. We were probably the only two who left the train, a discouraging sign. It was like going to a restaurant and you were the only customer. I looked around at the grubby station with great disappointment. "This is Tallahassee railroad station?", I said loudly. It was small and no where as beautiful as Sidi Gaber station, which is not even the main train station of Alexandria. Sidi Gaber was built with yellow stones, a plain but cheerful station. Immediately after leaving the station in the summer, you feel the breeze of the sea. No breeze was in Tallahassee station on that hot August day. In fact, it was very humid like I imagined the tropics to be. We were sweating profusely. It didn't help that we wore wool tailored suits with vests or that we were carrying those large heavy leather bags full of books. Egyptians generally assumed that going abroad, usually to Europe, meant going to a country of cold climate so we wore heavy clothes.

Here we were in this ugly train station when I spotted a reminder that we were nevertheless in Amreeka the Wonderland. It was a water fountain. None of these fountains existed in Egypt at the time. We were also thirsty so the site of the fountain was doubly exciting. Moreover, there was a choice since there were two fountains one labeled "White" and the other "Colored". Abdo started drinking from the "White" labeled fountain. I felt lucky that the other fountain was available to me. Who would go for a "White" water fountain when a "Colored" water fountain was available?" I told my friend. I wondered what color would come out, purple, red, yellow, or perhaps variable color like that magical horse in the Land of Oz. In any case, I am going to drink colored water like Kool-Aid. But, to my great disappointment, warm clear colorless water spouted at my face. "Wait a minute. What is going on here?".

I looked around. I found the same labels "White", "Colored" repeated on the rest room doors and station doors. So the color had nothing to do with the water, it had to do with the people. "Negroes" are colored and "Whites" are not. Here is one time when a "negative" is "positive". "Colorless is good and colored is bad". My heart sank to the bottom of my feet. This time was not because I was considered a "Negro" but because of the extent to which humans can be degraded because of the color of their skin. I was so deeply, but quietly upset. Colored or White water, I still looked forward to studying at Florida State University and I still dreamt of the swimming beauties, even though I was still dedicated to being loyal to my fiancé in Alexandria.

Finally, I had arrived in Amreeka: the Wonderland, the great Emerald City, the Land of Oz. However, contrary to my fantasies, Amreeka also had a bitter flavor.

EPISODE FIVE:

I Lost My Baby!

Exposure to a culture wildly different from one's own is like a big leap into a unique, peculiar, and strange zone not unlike Rod Sterling's "The Twilight Zone". Eyes, ears and nose were continuously engaged in seeing the unexpected, hearing different sounds, and smelling new aromas. Differences were particularly vivid then in the Fifties before globalization, thus falafel was eaten exclusively in the Middle East and hamburgers were eaten only in America. Those were the days my friend that we thought would never end when variety was abundant. Even within the USA, each state had some element or another which manifested a unique subculture. Unfortunately, now you can eat eggs rancheros, pizza, Thai food, Chinese food, Vietnamese food and Afghani food anywhere. Thus, part of the fun of traveling and visiting different places is gone thanks to commercial globalization. One should not complain too much; generations of the post-cloning era might well envy us for the varied features people currently have!

There I was with my Egyptian roommate in an efficiency apartment on College Avenue, closer to downtown Tallahassee than to campus. It was easy to walk the five or six blocks to the Chemistry building, except when it was raining heavily in the summer or freezing cold in the winter. That particular winter, my second since arrival, I was taking a graduate Chemistry course that started around seven a.m. One morning, after surmounting several barriers, getting up, dressing and walking to campus in freezing weather, I was not permitted in class. I was late by just a few minutes. Then these other

Egyptians who took the same class met the same fate. We were all walking together. It was funny because we constituted two thirds of the class. I must admit, however, that I was never late for the rest of the semester. It is true that the instructor, freshly graduated, was obnoxious, but he was a good teacher. I got a bad grade on the first test, but somehow I ended up with an "A" which was well earned, not necessarily for the effort exerted, but for the suffering involved having to brave freezing temperatures for which even my Egyptian-tailored wool suit was not suited for at all. I thought we were correct, after all, assuming that going abroad meant going to a cold country. I guess we somehow assumed that there were no seasons except winter! In northern Florida, summer could be sizzling hot and extremely humid, worst than the hottest days in Alexandria. It is amazing how we, from afar, often look at a country or even a whole continent monolithically and stereotypically. We have stereotyped the weather!

At that time, I was learning with fondness about American culture. I was attempting many activities, and acquiring different tastes in food and clothing. I remember buying a suit, which had a light blue color, what I called in French "blue ciel". No, I did not speak French, though I studied the language for four years, but in Egypt at that time it was in vogue, i.e., "tres chic", to throw out a few French words. It impressed others at the time. This lingers on among the old generation, but has faded among the young generation who now use American lingo. Anyhow, I was happy to wear my newly acquired " bleu ciel " suit, and a red bow tie (papillon) and look "tres" American.

Naturally, I fell into various traps and gimmicks. I was offered a "special deal" for magazine subscriptions (Post, Look, Coronet, etc...) with the usual attractive features, such as an additional free magazine subscription if you subscribe to four. I was not used to the idea of a well dressed salesman knocking on your door and explaining an offer in the most attractive terms. It was difficult to say no, though later I learned and even enjoyed to say "no thank you", particularly to insurance agents and salesmen and religious zealots spreading the gospel! I started receiving the magazines regularly. I hardly read them seriously. Being in graduate school, I had no time to read magazines.

Between qualifying exams, various courses, preparing for foreign languages exams, reading scientific literature, doing research, attending seminars, and taking care of personal things such as shopping, laundry and cleaning the apartment, there was hardly any time but to briefly glance at the university paper, the Flambeau, and the local paper, the Tallahassee Democrat. Perhaps there were brief moments to look at some photos especially of beautiful women in Look and Life magazines. All these magazines quickly piled up and I had to carry them every time I moved, which was not infrequent. I guess I was certain that I would eventually have time to look through them, or perhaps it was the guilt of spending all that money without reading them. Obviously, I over estimated the time available, something I keep advising my son not to do without much success. I do not remember when or where I disposed of these magazines, but I am certain it was an agonizing decision.

I was always surprised at the amount of advertisements that took a sizable portion of each magazine. In fact, it was, and still is, irritating to keep going past all the advertisement to locate an article to read. I quickly learned that here in America, advertisement and commercials are an important element and even a central part of American life. I was astonished that several formal courses were given in advertisement. The notion of commercials in radio and television programs was a new phenomenon to me. What was striking was that, even then, politics and religion had a strong commercial component. Well this is America. I often recalled my first ever glance at a TV in a hotel lounge in New York City the very first morning on American soil.

We did not have television at that time in Egypt, and we relied heavily on radio. We still had a very old fashioned radio, certainly bigger in size than any TV I had seen thus far. It was Italian made and was a source of immense pleasure for the family, well most of the family. My father barely listened to the radio, except for important news, such as the removal of King Farouk, or the ascendancy of Gamal Abdel Nasser to power, or the failed assassination attempt on his life. The rest of the family stayed up late to hear a movie broadcast on radio. Listening to a movie was quite an experience. There always was an experienced commentator who helped the listeners follow the movie by making brief remarks once in a while, such as, "Now Hassan is warmly kissing her," or "The thief is climbing through the window. He is now searching for the safe." We heard comedies, as well as dramas. Often, we had seen the movie before. That gave us a special taste in listening and imagining the scenes. With the visual senses at rest, the brain becomes active in visualizing the scenes. I am sure that different brains visualized scenes differently, even though we were hearing the same movie. This is not particularly peculiar, for in a real movie with a serious story reactions are different. Reactions are the net result of coupling between the movie as projected, and the personality and experiences of the viewer. The anticipated pleasure of expecting the broadcast of a movie, was sometimes quenched when my father prohibited us from staying up late, although we sneaked out of our beds, squeezed ourselves as close to the radio as possible, and hoped that our father was sound asleep.

My grandfather was an avid listener of the radio. He especially enjoyed the female singer Um Kalthoum, the Arab World's premiere vocalist. It was like an obsession that I could not comprehend. My grandmother often teased him about her. Um Kalthoum was already famous and was quickly becoming a legend. From Morocco and Tunisia to Iraq and Yemen, Arabs everywhere eagerly awaited her monthly performances. Some of the wealthy flew into Cairo especially to hear her in person. Years earlier, my grandfather had gone regularly to her performances, and being blind, he was always accompanied by his oldest son. She sang Arabic poetry mostly around the theme of love, patriotic songs, poetry praising Prophet Mohammad, and also sang another on the occasion of King Farouk's birthday. Her long songs of love poetry, such as Omar Alkhayam's, drove the crowd into a state of ecstasy. She had an unprecedented voice and was able to use her remarkable vocal cords to produce the notes and emotions she required. Now, I quite appreciate her love songs, and often dwell into the meaning of the poem, reaching a level of ecstasy, which I did not feel before. Perhaps the poetic love expressed by Um Kalthoum is the elusive true love.

As a young man I only appreciated some of her short love songs. As a matter of fact, one of her songs became my love song. It said: "If you are in love why deny it? Love appears in the eyes of lovers," or in Arabic, "Madam teheb betenker leeh, dallee yeheb yeban fi aineeh." I was more fond of another young upcoming singer, Abdel Haleem Hafez. I used to sing one of his popular songs to my fiancé. "The beautiful is my life, what shall I tell her?" El helw hayaati wrouhy waoolo aih?"

In Tallahassee we could not yet afford to have a TV set. Besides, we were not quite settled, so we relied on the radio. I listened from time to time, especially on the weekends. However, you cannot imagine the irritation I endured each time the program was interrupted by commercials. This also applied to television when I had an occasion to view it. One song I was attracted to because of the music and the voice of Tennessee Ernie Ford was "Sixteen Tons". At first I did not comprehend the lyrics, but hearing it repeatedly, I quickly appreciated its significance, and I was surprised that a song which was clearly critical of one of the corner stones of the American system could be aired. It was especially surprising that in the Fifties, "the communist menace period", that song became so popular that over one million records were sold, and was the fastest selling single in the history of the Capitol Record Company. Recalling the words may underline what I mean:

> *Some people say a man is made out of mud,*
> *A poor man's made out of muscle and blood,*
> *Muscle and blood, skin and bones...*
> *A mind that's weak and a back that's strong,*
> *You load sixteen tons, and what do you get?*
> *Another day older and deeper in debt,*
> *St. Peter, don't you call me, 'cause I can't go,*
> *I owe my soul to the company store.*

It was more interesting to hear the song after I have learned that it was inspired by a letter lamenting the death of a journalist killed while covering combat during World War II, and from comments of an old coal miner in reference to "scrip" money advanced by the coal company for food bought by the miners. This song had a profound effect on me, raising the barriers to buy anything on credit. My record after forty years is quite impressive, or is it? After all, I had car payments, mortgage payments and a few other items were on credit, so in a way, I still owed part of my soul to the company store.

I guess I have a particular affinity to songs in any language, with deep meaning. I am fond of attempting to transmit the ecstasy I feel when hearing such a song to special friends who do not know the language, a challenging task, but a fulfilling one. One such song is performed by Um Kalthoum, in which the poet describes her lover in the following words:

This world is a book you in it are the thought,
This world is nights, you in it are life,
This world is eyes you in it are the sight,
This world is a sky you in it are the moon.

The lyrics, combined with the music, and above all, the voice and the performance of Um Kalthoum produce a state that we call in Arabic "Nashwa", which is simply ecstasy, that caused the audience to shout demanding repetitions. Another verse of the same song that simply drove the audience into a frenzy says: "Tomorrow may be beautiful, but the present is more beautiful". That may explain my characterization of Um Kalthoum as the "Professor of Love".

During the first few weeks of living in America, I kept hearing a song in the morning that caused me sadness and depression. I couldn't believe that people could enjoy listening in the morning to a song that mourns the death of a child. I kept listening attentively, but kept getting the same horrid meaning. To rationalize all this, I convinced myself it must be an element of the weirdness of Americans. The song starts something like this: "One morning I lost my baby. I almost lost my mind". Finally I had the courage to ask an American friend about this depressing song. He laughed and explained that the baby in the song is not a child, but another variety of a baby. I still did not like the "baby" expression, however the original feeling of weirdness was tempered since at least the song became comprehensible. Till now, I am still not used to the expression. Why in the world would you call a woman you love "baby"? Long before the feminist movement, I kind of felt that this implies some diminution of women. On reflection, however, I thought of some Egyptian song lyrics and I was amazed at how weird and even ridiculous some of them are, especially for carriers of other cultures. Listen to this: "What does love produce except wailing?" "Eelhob feeh aih gheir elnooh"; "Love without hope is the epitome of love" "Elhob men gheir amal asma maany elgharam"; or "Oh, the slipper of my lover, I wish I were you"." Ya shebsheb elhanaa yaretny kont anaa".

Till this day, I try to imitate Tennessee Ernie Ford's distinctive voice, without much luck in "I owe my soul to the company stooore". I must also admit that I am even fond, out of sheer nostalgia, of repeating: "One morning I lost my baby, I almost lost my mind".

EPISODE SIX:

John Boardman

It must have been the first few weeks in Tallahassee. I was in that strange enjoyable zone where all my senses were particularly receptive. Every smell, gesture, sound and scene was new and had a special impact on me. I was amenable to new ideas and was quite willing to try different activities and consider different ways of thinking. I was completely "free" and independent. Of course, I had my set of principles that served as my anchors, and my self-imposed forbidden zones. I had lots to learn. My two Egyptian colleagues, Ali and Mostafa, who had been at FSU for almost two years automatically became my mentors and friends. Their knowledge of the environment, the language and habits seemed infinite at the time. They served as the experts with whom I consulted on various matters and they were willingly helpful. Ali, Mostafa, Abdo and I quickly became like four musketeers on campus. We would go together for registration, attend chemistry seminars, shopping, to the barber, to football games and to the movies. We often met at the Coke machine in the chemistry department drinking and laughing almost perpetually. Other graduate students, mostly Americans, were amused, perhaps puzzled at the constant laughter and assumed that Egyptians are always jovial. Well, most generalizations are inaccurate but there is some truth in them. In fact, most other Arabs acknowledge Egyptians' sense of humor, wild jokes and joviality.

One night, Ali and Mostafa were invited to a party by a graduate student in physics. Naturally they asked Abdo and myself to join them. To me, the concept of a party was new: a gathering where fifteen to twenty individuals meet, many of them hardly knowing each other. They are crowded in a room with drinks, some food, (nothing fantastic) and some peanuts (fancy nuts like macadamia, almond, pistachio or hazel nuts were unavailable or out of reach for graduate students with assistantships of one hundred forty dollars per month). We were thrown together simultaneously talking, listening to music, eating and drinking in a noisy atmosphere clouded with smoke, punctuated with expressions of joy, mostly artificial, contrived laughter, or screams of "yahoos" and "yippies". For me, the atmosphere was both strange and amusing. At one corner of the room I had some conversation with our host, John Boardman, a tall fellow, awkward in the way he moves and carries himself. Some may call him a "nerd" in today's terminology. He told me that he is a graduate student in physics, that he is Jewish and that he considers himself a liberal. At that time people were divided as segregationists and integrationists, and liberals fell in the latter category. John impressed me with his vast general knowledge, beyond his specialization in physics, which I thought unusual especially since this broad knowledge included the history and culture of foreign lands. As an Egyptian who was involved in student political activities for many years in high school and university, I considered myself quite knowledgeable as far as the Egyptian political map. I thought I certainly knew more than him in this category. I was wrong. He brought up a number of issues and names of political leaders that gave me the impression that he knew a lot, especially when he supported his information by referring to specific pages from books that he grabbed from his extensive library collection. Many of his books were paperbacks, arranged on wooden shelves supported by bricks, another novelty to me that attracted my attention which I would imitate later. He discussed the political stands of Nahhas Pasha, a former Egyptian Prime Minister who headed the most important political party in Egypt before the Nasser era. He addressed me as Ashraf Effendi, a title given to junior educated persons. I was quite impressed with John Boardman's knowledge and I was determined to expand and deepen my knowledge of America, my country's history and beyond. After exchanging many "hellos", "how are yous" and "nice to meet yous" the party was over. My face was strained by my constant smiling.

In America, I was told that smiling is a necessary gesture that makes one liked. In fact, I noticed several signs and slogans urging people to smile. Students in the streets and waitresses had a constant smile on their faces which I thought was very pleasant. Nevertheless, I felt uncomfortable with my face strained from smiling constantly. On the other hand, that helped me to mingle with people and be able to at least appear able to converse and listen, even though I did not understand half of what was being said because of accents, strange words and, simply, limited language ability.

A few weeks, perhaps a few months, passed by and I read about John in the student newspaper, the Flambau. The Dean of Students, a rather chubby likable person who bears a close resemblance to a film star who appeared as a kind father in many musicals of those days, announced that John was expelled from the university. He was not caught smoking marijuana, raping a woman on campus or cheating in an exam. Absolutely not. His shameful deed was that he broke one of the most important sacred social rules: He invited a few African students, mostly Nigerians, from Florida A&M University, which was known then as the Negro college. Florida A&M is in the same town, but in a neighborhood that we seldom passed by.

It was amazing to me how two societies could live together yet not interact, just like two immiscible liquids. A sharp demarcation line, like that which separates oil and water. That does not mean that a few molecules of oil do not wander into the water phase and visa versa but they soon get trapped back to their phase. Thus black maids took care of white babies in a white neighborhood and black janitors worked at Florida State University. But there was no interaction between the two schools of higher learning.

Once in a while we heard of the much better football team of Florida Agriculture & Mechanical University, FAMU. Florida State had a miserable football team that was regularly defeated every year by the Universities of Florida, Georgia, Georgia Tech, etc... The music band of Florida A&M had a particularly colorful uniform. They were envied for their football team and their colorful band. The two Tallahassee teams never played against each other even though teams from other states came all the way to play with the mediocre Florida State team, and Florida A&M traveled long distances to get defeated by other teams. What is more strange is how an alien like me who has nothing to do with the history of racial hatred and discrimination accepted in reality, if not intellectually, such an odd situation. Was it acceptance or, more accurately, considering the matter not an immediate concern specially that I was a foreigner who came to study? Florida A&M was to me like the locked room in a huge house that was forbidden to enter. Mythology shrouded the room with mystery and fear but also inspired abundant curiosity. I was satisfied with voicing my opposition from time to time, which irritated some. I remember a young Canadian student whom I dated a few times stopped seeing me because of this. I identified myself as being Egyptian and not "Negro". Perhaps it was a self-defense mechanism, lest I would be identified as belonging to a group designated by the white majority as being inferior. Every time I had to fill an application in the university or for a driver's license, I would be perplexed by the reductionist definitions of race: Negro or White (Caucasian). According to US officials, Egyptians were formally identified as Caucasian, otherwise we would not have been admitted to FSU. This posed a contradiction to me, I felt I was not "Negro", yet as an Egyptian I am certainly African, I do not have white skin and I am happy with my color. The whole idea of race classification and its implications was repugnant to me. Such initial feeling later evolved to a clear outward opposition to all forms of discrimination, racism included.

Mr. Boardman's crime was inviting a number of Nigerian students who were studying at Florida A&M. Some neighbors, white of course, were angry and called the police. The cops, all white of course, quickly arrived and promptly dismissed every one, roughed up some of the guests and obviously the white rebel whom they considered a "discredit to his race". I do not know if his identity as a Jew was known to the police. That would have made matters even worse. I knew at the time signs such as "No Dogs, No Negroes, No Jews" were still found in the South. I do not remember the exact order, but it was ironic to see a poor run down hotel posting such a sign.

At the time I was confused; are Jews individuals who adhere to Judaism or are they a race? In any case, are Semites white or colored? It was puzzling! My puzzlement was tempered by the fact that there is another division, Yankee and Southerner or Confederate, hurrah, hurrah! So "Whites" can be against each other also. There is also another distinction, Protestant vs. Catholic with the latter being somewhat bad according to the former. I also learned that Protestants are further divided into Southern Baptists, Methodists, Lutherans, etc...

John was defended by some on the ground that those he invited are not "Negroes" of the American variety. They were Africans and "foreign" students, but many did not buy this feeble argument. After all, American "Negroes" were originally Africans when they were captured and enslaved. Some even argued that at least American Negroes are partly American. Others argued that these Nigerian Negroes are not a threat. They are foreigners and will soon leave, but the other Negroes are locals and are potential polluters of the white race. These contradictions reminded me with a similar one in my own country. A Muslim Egyptian studying abroad returning with a British or American wife does not create a problem, on the contrary the family may boast about the marriage even though the bride is Christian. If, however, a Muslim marries a Christian Egyptian (Copt), which is permitted in Islam, all hell breaks loose!

I do not recall that the student body protested John Boardman's dismissal. There may have been some faculty who protested, but I do not remember any. It would be interesting to go back to the pages of the Flambeau or the Tallahassee Democrat to check that. In fact, I'd love to do that to find out who dared at the time.

Today it is politically correct to be ashamed of actions that may be considered racist, but what is in the heart is in the heart. However, one should not belittle such an initial step. For some individuals may start by adopting politically correct slogans superficially at first then evolve through self education to a more genuine conviction which may be transmitted to the new generation. For others, it is a dead end path since they stop at the level of mechanical conformity.

I must say, I admired John Boardman then, and I admire him more now. He was genuine. Action identifies the authentic and exposes the fake. Where is John Boardman now and what does he believe? I do not know. Is he still authentic or is he a millionaire busy multiplying his fortune? Since I believe that he was genuine in his beliefs I prefer to imagine him as a college professor somewhere, teaching Physics and challenging injustice as well.

EPISODE SEVEN:

The Seminoles and Other Mania

First experiences are always exciting and novel. Of course, most first experiences happen in earlier years of life and are forgotten. No one remembers the first time eating chocolate or licking ice cream unless parents recorded such thrilling moments. Being a grandfather, I have witnessed such moments like watching my granddaughter seeing the sea for the first time as she gazed at the vast sea and the waves coming and crashing on shore perpetually. She was mesmerized and kept looking silently in amazement. There are memories of such moments if they happen when we are adults like the first kiss, the first heart beat signaling falling in love and the first aero plane ride.

Traveling has that effect, especially if the country visited is very different culturally and visually. Coming to the US had such an impact on me. So going to a college football game for the first time was a special experience. I was excited and had no clue what to expect, except that it was like rugby which I had seen glimpses of in British movies. I assumed that American football was similar. I also was puzzled why it was called football since feet are rarely used in the game. Watching the game on a screen is radically different from being in the stadium. The game is only one aspect of the show, which includes all sort of spectacles: the cheer leaders and their acrobatics and sexy outfits, the slogans they shout and we repeat, going to the concession stand to buy drinks and hot dogs, the tension when the entire game hangs on a kick or a final attempt, and a long pass or a fast run for a touchdown that brings us to our feet or causing big disappointment depending on which team scored. Being in the stadium and hearing the sounds and the impact of players pounding each other reminded me with gladiators in Roman times as seen in movies. I was surprised by the extent of violence in the game, which reminded me with my shock when I first saw a bull attacking a horse during a bull fight with his eyes gazing in pain that caused the screaming of my daughter. Much later, my son became interested in playing football, and was obsessed with certain stars like Terry Bradshaw and Franco Harris. I persuaded him, or more accurately, aborted his dream of becoming a football player. Recent knowledge of severe and more subtle long term injuries, especially concussions, vindicated my decision.

One gets obsessed with the desire of winning for the Seminoles, the FSU team, as if it represented me personally, and its winning is like personal glory even though, back then, the chances for the Seminoles to win was so slim, but it was good to hope and expect a miracle. In one game the fortunes of the Seminoles changed many times, which added to the excitement.

Going to the game, finding a parking place for the huge Buick that my Egyptian friend had, walking the remaining distance to Campbell's Stadium, watching cheerleaders, and shouting "We Want a Touchdown!!", which rarely came, or "Hold That Line!!", which was rarely held, and leaving the game, watching people drink like crazy and prepare for fraternity parties and sorority parties was a strange, unusual and fresh experience. One highlight of the spectacle was the music band during the game and, at halftime, it was amusing watching the leader marching with his back bent backward with his fancy outfit. Unfortunately, the games were associated with lots of drinking and misbehavior. One incident was not pleasant when one person threatened us with a pistol because Ali blocked his car where we parked. That was scary, and it did not help that we were foreigners as he cussed and used racial epitaphs. Loud parties at fraternities and sororities, as well as student apartments with booze pouring and laughter were expected at every home game. One young drunk student was singing "I am a wreck from Georgia Tech."

The Seminoles played poorly at the time. Little did we know that they will become the number one team in the nation decades later. As a matter of fact, the Florida A&M team, which was labeled the "negro" team, played better, but they never played the white FSU team. Their band was more colorful in all aspects! I even joined a group of chemistry graduate students who occasionally played touch football and I enjoyed it. I quickly became addicted to professional football viewing. For an unknown reason, I became a fan of the Baltimore Colts, and was amazed at the precise fourth down short passes of Johnny Unitas at critical moments leading to an impossible victory that was thrilling. At the time, I did not give attention to the fact that the name Seminoles referred to an Indian tribe.

At the time, I knew little about Native Americans and that little was, unfortunately, derived from American movies. In movies, Native Americans were mostly depicted as violent people eager to cut scalps of white settlers. Very little was mentioned about their misfortunes at the hands of the white man. The only Native American who had some humanity and wisdom was the one helping the white man encroaching on his tribe. Opposite to him was an ugly native who invariably had a scared face and was a war monger. I must admit that I partly swallowed such images. Only recently, a few movies such as "Dancing with Wolves" had a more realistic image of such a humanistic culture. The Seminoles endured long wars for forty years and were forced to move further west. I learned much later from reading about the plight of Native Americans, including interesting information about Black Seminoles who escaped slavery and joined the Seminoles.

The Seminoles nickname was adopted after it became a coed institution eight years before I came. I must say that I enjoyed the show before each game at Doak Campbell Stadium when a student with brown face paint and wearing a costume similar to Native American Chief Osceola with a garnet bandana and carrying a feathered spear arrived riding a colorful horse, "Renegade". The game started by him hurling a burning spear into the ground at midfield. The issue of such depiction is opposed by some. However, a much greater opposition is currently against the use of the name "Redskins" for the professional football team in Washington. I predict that name will be changed, and when that happens some expect the fortunes of the team will improve. We will see.

Football was a weekly activity in the fall, but there were other attractions. I once went with my Australian friend, who liked gambling, to a dog race. Dog racing was so amusing that I started laughing when the guy announced "Here Comes Rusty!", the mechanical rabbit that the dogs would try to catch. My friend lost a few, but came out winning a few bucks. I guess I was exploring Americana activities and craziness. Horse racing seemed okay, but dog racing makes one pause and then ask "why not?" How about camel racing? I find it very amusing to watch thoroughbred camels race sometimes with and other times without a rider. Some Arab TV stations feature such races.

Aside from sport activities, I remember going for the first time, and many times afterwards, to the drive-in theater. What an exciting idea! How come we don't have drive-in theaters in Egypt even though the weather is perfect for this? One of the attractions of drive-ins is the privacy of your car to kiss and neck and to do other enjoyable things. How about drive-in restaurants and those beautiful girls in tiny shorts, if you can still call them short, some on roller skates, others with cowboy hats, and serving banana splits or sundaes.

I have pleasant memories of the nearly six years I spent at Florida State University, or FSU, often pronounced F-Esh-U, one year as a bachelor and the rest as a married couple.

EPISODE EIGHT:

Fousin and Mousin: A Modest Contribution to the English Language

I never thought that I would ever make a unique contribution to the English language. English is neither my mother tongue nor my father tongue, but my contribution emanated from necessity. Whenever the word "uncle" or "aunt" came up in a conversation with my American friends, it led me to add whether the uncle or the aunt was from the mother's or father's side. To an Egyptian, this makes a big difference; the two varieties of uncles and aunts have distinct flavors. They almost belong to different species, socially speaking.

According to our culture, the uncle who is the father's brother, named *ammo* or *ammy* in Arabic, is usually serious, not easily accessible, respected, even a bit feared, and not particularly liked. The uncle from the mother's side, called *khalo* or *khali* in Arabic, is often delightful, loving, more intimate and informal. There is even a well-known Egyptian saying which states, "The boy takes after his khalo".

Wondering about such distinctions has all sorts of cultural implications. In the Egyptian culture, uncles, whether *ammos* or *khalos*, are important members of the family. We see them often, unlike in Western societies, where visiting uncles or aunts is not as frequent an event. They are involved in decision making processes of the family. Moreover, the distinction between *ammo* and *khalo* reflects the relative positions of the father and mother in the family, and more generally, men and women in society. The father is the ruler, or at least the presumed ruler of the family, and its policy maker. The mother is supposedly the obedient implementer of those policies, with some unauthorized alterations allowed, hidden or simply ignored. Traditionally, fathers must appear stern and serious but mothers do not have to put on such a façade. Mothers often act as intermediaries to soften the father's hasty or harsh decisions and to make such decrees wiser and more practical. This prescribed mode of interaction applies generally, regardless of the status of the family. Of course, this cultural prescription collapses if the same person is a khalo and an ammo. Sometimes, however, the same person acts as expected of him, loosening up when he is a khalo and being more serious when his role is ammo. I wonder sometimes if my behavior is different with my nieces and nephews or perhaps they relate to me differently as they associate me with a father or a mother.

Aside from philosophizing and analyzing, I asked myself, "Wouldn't it be convenient and useful if the English language, which suffers in my opinion from such linguistic vagueness in deciphering uncles, were to be remedied?" Each language incorporates several new words anyway, not only because of new scientific discoveries and technologies but political and cultural developments also inject novel expressions. Words such as: DNA, MRI, VHS, DVD, IT, PDF, virtual reality, cyberspace, cellular phone and so on are now commonly used. An essentially new language popped up because of the Internet and the Web. The other day, my granddaughter challenged me if I could decipher several abbreviations used on internet chats, such as: sya, ttyl, lol, brb,..etc.

Here is my remarkable and, at the same time, simple and easy to remember suggestion that will revolutionize the English language, will have a positive impact on family relations, will eliminate social ills and will also secure peace in our time along with a place for my name in history. I will keep the word "uncle", but will preface it with an "f" for a father's brother and with an "m" for a mother's brother. Voila! Two new words are born: "funcle" for *a'ammo* and "muncle" for *khalo*. After a while, you get used to it. Even the computer, which does not recognize these new words, soon will. But why not extend the logic to cousins, and invent two more words. A "fousin" is a cousin from the father's side, and a "mousin" is the other type. Likewise, there are two types of aunts, a "fant" and a "mant".

Those who advocate family values whether sincerely, or politically, should be elated. Who knows, perhaps the Republican as well as the Democratic Party will compete in advocating the usage of these new words in a novel attempt to improve their family values credentials! The introduction and usage of "funcle", "muncle", "fousin" and "mousin"," fant" and "mant" should usher a return to the extended family concept with all its glorious results. The computer screens and cellular telephones will buzz with the new words. "My fousin is visiting for a week. She is not my favorite but I have to persevere". "My rich funcle is stingy, and would not loan me a few thousand dollars." "Unfortunately, my muncle is generous, but poor, or is he poor because he is generous? What is the meaning of a generous, poor person anyway? I will try again with my funcle. Maybe I will ask my fant to persuade my funcle, but please do not mention this to my fousins and mousins".

EPISODE NINE:

A Private Matter

John Heisman was a postdoctoral fellow in a group headed by a well known scientist, Hans Gaffron. Florida State University tried hard to have him move his group and relocate to Tallahassee. The university considered the move a big coup which would put FSU in the forefront of biological research. Hans Gaffron was a prominent German research scientist in the area of photosynthesis. He left Nazi Germany in protest of fascism and moved to the University of Chicago. His petite charming German wife, Clara, was also a main supervisor in his lab. Mr. Troll was a head technician and the true engine in the lab. Both of them were kind of parents to Soo Soo.

Gaffron made interesting and important discoveries in the quest of unraveling the secrets of the crucial phenomenon of photosynthesis, the basis of life on our planet. As the name implies, it is a synthetic process that uses light photons. It is an ingenious natural process by which carbon dioxide, which we exhale and is abundant in our atmosphere, can be transferred into starch and produces oxygen as well. The key to this process is light energy and the remarkable chlorophyll molecule that imparts the beautiful green color to plants. Hundreds of scientists invested millions of hours to understand the molecular mechanisms of this efficient process that we hope to mimic to store solar energy and achieve a truly clean energy source and avoid destroying our fragile environment.

My wife, Soo Soo had just finished her bachelor's degree in bacteriology and was appointed as a technical research assistant in Gaffron's lab. She was excited about her work and took it seriously as she always takes any task, trivial or important. In addition, our financial situation radically improved and moved us from the category of being in debt and having to worry about our dwindling food supply at the end of the month and borrowing money to a situation where we actually began to save every month. Barbara, the wife of another chemistry graduate student, worked in the same lab and became a friend to Soheir. Soheir liked Mrs. Gaffron even though she drove others in the lab crazy in the course of her supervision. Soheir's direct supervisor was a young professor who was rather stiff and socially awkward. There was also a young postdoctoral fellow in the lab, John Heisman.

John invited us once to his apartment for dinner. He shared the apartment with a male roommate. Both made a special effort to prepare a sophisticated meal. My recollection is that neither the company nor the meal was anything big. I remember distinctly the uneasy feeling I had, perhaps because I did not know most of the guests. I had noticed the abundance of pictures of nude women on the walls of the apartment.

My uneasiness was certainly not that nude women were displayed. Viewing artistic nude photos of beautiful women had always delighted me even though that may be considered now as sexist or politically incorrect. On that occasion, I just felt that the display of nude photos was overdone and thus contrived.

I always reacted negatively to any sign of being pretentious. I remember an Egyptian relative of mine, Tant Tou Tou, who did not know any English, yet she punctuated her speech with English words such as "excuse me" which she pronounced in a funny way like "excuz me". I was always fascinated how a poor person would attempt to over dress and to give top priority to appearance or how a poor Black American living literally in a shack had a polished used Cadillac or Buick with bright colors in front of the shack. This is not unlike a person who repeatedly and annoyingly uses words like "comrade", "hallelujah" or "insha-allah" (God willing in Arabic) to display his or her Marxist or religious credentials, respectively, or like a teenager who never touched the cheeks of a woman but frequently boasts about his wild Casanova-like conquests and adventures. In a similar vein, I remember a graduate student who was a classmate in a difficult quantum chemistry course. He requested from our professor to give him references of the original German papers since he knew German well. Those of us who were taking the course were really intimidated. To our shock and amusement as well, he flunked the course. He received not a D but an F; so much for our totally unfounded intimidation. I developed a keen sense of suspicion for all acts of pretension.

Weeks passed and I totally forgot the meal and the gallery of nude photos until a certain event that occurred a few weeks later. At the time, my activities as a chemistry graduate student, particularly my research, dominated my life. I used to spend long hours in the lab performing or preparing for future experiments that required clever designs to unravel some scientific puzzles or to answer important questions. The work was exciting and hours passed so quickly. I had a close friend, Mike O'Dwyer. Our friendship was perhaps an unlikely one. He is from Australia of Irish dissent, Catholic; in fact his sister is a Catholic nun. He used to observe eating fish on Fridays and would check lists of movies that had his church's seal of approval though he saw many films that were not on the list with a mixture of joy and guilt. He had a solid background in mathematics and physics so he passed all necessary examinations easily, besides he was a meticulous experimentalist; I learned a lot from him. We enjoyed each other's company; we would talk, gossip, criticize, admire, despise, laugh, agree and disagree. Most of this occurred after leaving the lab, usually at the early hours of the following morning. We would drive in Mike's very old Ford to the Bus Stop at the top of the hill on College Avenue. The Bus Stop was a tiny diner that served coffee, root beer, eggs and waffles and was always crowded. It took only a few men to crowd the tiny place. It was fun and I enjoyed going there after a long night in the lab before returning home. Our visits to the Bus Stop were frequent and, besides, where else could you go at two or three in the morning?

I used to regularly read both the Tallahassee Democrat and the Flambeau, the university paper. One morning, both papers reported the shocking news that a number of homosexuals who regularly met at the Bus Stop were arrested, and among them was a postdoctoral fellow at the university whose name I immediately recognized as that of John Heisman. My God! We often went to that Bus Stop. Frankly, I did not observe anything unusual. Remember it was the late Fifties. No one would dare display homosexuality. By contrast, exhibiting heterosexuality was apparently encouraged, judging from the scenes of intense necking around women's dorms around closing time at eleven pm. No one would imagine that a time would come when "Gay Pride" would be a slogan and gay parades and gay rights would exist and be politically correct.

On reading the paper, my reaction was that of shock, fear and relief. Shock that we unwittingly frequented a homosexual gathering spot, fear that we could have been easily suspected of being homosexuals and relief that we were not there that night. I do not remember feeling any sense of sympathy or anger. In fact, I did not give the matter much thought except the possibility of being wrongly involved or suspected.

Immediately there were calls at FSU for firing John Heisman. It would not have become an issue if his Professor Gaffron had taken the easy way out and terminated his research appointment. However, on principle Gaffron adamantly refused to do that. He left Nazi Germany and protested against fascism and would not fire a person because of a sexual preference different from the majority of the society. However repulsive the homosexual act may have been to heterosexuals of the time, that was not the issue. The issue was individual privacy and also the separation between an individual's public personal life and his or her private life.

Gaffron stood his ground and finally prevailed in the face of immense opposition and John Heisman remained with the university. I recognized, acknowledged and supported Gaffron's principled stand. The real test of one's belief in support of individual rights and beliefs is when one is confronted with a situation when those beliefs are counter to one's own, or as in this case, when it involves an activity one considers abhorrent or repulsive. I admired Gaffron for his consistency and intellectual honesty.

The event made me think about the question of where I stand. I could not avoid the issue, since I saw John Heisman during seminars and other occasions. It was obvious that many avoided sitting beside him, which must have been tormenting for him. I was put to the test when he sat beside me during a seminar. I simply could not imitate others and move to another seat. That would have been utterly wrong and indecent. Besides, such an act would have reflected sexual insecurity on my part. Thoughts raced in my mind and finally a firm decision materialized. I did not move from my seat, I thought one had to be sensitive to others' feelings. Even then, I was convinced that his sexual preference is a private matter.

EPISODE TEN:

It Takes a Village:
Unraveling The Knot

In my early days in Tallahassee, I met a handsome Arab from Syria who came from an upper middle class family. His father was a doctor who was supporting his son's education at FSU. He took courses in education, social science and humanities. In no way would his course make-up lead to a pre-medical background. However, he led his father to believe that he was preparing himself to follow in his father's footsteps as a doctor and, thus, inherit the family practice and clinic. He was not particularly serious about his studies. His love of photography was a priority. With his fancy camera he took some nice photos and some were indeed artistic and beautiful.

Recently, while flipping through my old albums, I saw a photo of him with a group of friends during a New Year's party. The photograph immediately triggered my memory and time was instantly reversed. For a moment I was living again in the mid-Fifties and the brain restlessly scans events, music and sounds. A time window opens and one does not know what one may expect to see as part of the brain digs, perhaps randomly, into one of the files of the stored memory. Memories are never erased. They are waiting to be tapped and once one scene appears several other scenes start rolling. Flashbacking is an autocatalytic phenomenon.

I remember him as a handsome, shy fellow, very kind and friendly, rather silly sometimes, and even childish. He had many girlfriends, most of whom were beautiful, and most women adored him. But, I noticed that often they lost interest in him after a while. Being the President of the International Club, the foreign student club at FSU, I got to know some of these women. One of them had a crush on him, she confided in me that he is a delightful fellow, but his only obsession, with emphasis on only, was to take photos. By the way, some of these photos were semi-nude or completely nude. I used to kid him on the issue, telling him that girls like him but they are jealous from his damn camera. He loved girls too, obviously there was a barrier!

One evening, he explained why his fascination with women stops at photographing them and their beautiful bodies. Back in Syria when he reached adolescence, his father came up with a brilliant idea! Since he reached puberty his father thought he must be initiated in having sex. Rather than introducing him to some sexual education through some members of the family since there was a void in sex education books, he instead took him to a prostitute house for his first lesson in sexual intercourse. Sometimes this approach works, although in other situations the results could be disastrous in different ways. The boy was so scared and nervous that it was over before he had even begun. The woman slapped him and insulted him and instantly his sexual inhibitions developed. Such a failure created a barrier needed to be crushed before enjoying love making.

It is amazing how sexual attitudes reflect, both directly and subtly, cultural, religious and psychological events and concepts, and how easily barriers may be erected that are difficult to surmount or penetrate. In his case, his father didn't have religious taboos about sex, but his concept of sex probably reflected a mechanical approach and lack of respect and tenderness to women. His father's approach to sex education closed doors instead of opening one and a knot had tightly developed.

One summer, he disappeared from Tallahassee. "Where were you?" I asked when he returned. "I was in New York", he replied. I noticed immediately a different attitude, confident gestures and even his body language had been altered somehow. "What happened?", I asked with a probing smile. A glitter in his eyes said it all, "You had sex with a woman in New York". He blushed a bit and his radiant face had a broad smile.

Yes, he met a woman in Greenwich Village and, after one or two dry dates and tens of photos, some completely nude, she insisted on moving in with him and declared emphatically that she would sleep with him no matter what. All escape routes had been blocked and an assault of sexual education became imminent. The result was magnificent, he was finally liberated, a knot had been untied, inhibition had collapsed and he had become free, free at last! Borrowing the title of Hillary Clinton, it took a village to liberate him. In this case it was Greenwich Village.

EPISODE ELEVEN:

Blakely, Georgia

Soheir and I got an invitation, via the Foreign Students Advisor, to visit the Rotary Club in Blakely, Georgia. We spent a couple of days as guests of a rich family that practically owned Blakely. I was asked to speak to the Club about the political situation in Egypt. At these times I got some invitations to talk about one aspect or another about Egypt. It was too early, being a starting graduate student, to receive invitations to give science lectures. The only talks I gave were related to academic requirements. I was always delighted to talk about Egypt, so we were happy to accept the invitation to talk in Blakely.

We were told that Blakely was nicknamed the "Peanut Capital of the World". It was named after an Irish immigrant by the name of Captain Johnston Blakely who was famous for capturing a British ship. However, he and the ship, the Wasp, disappeared at sea. The small population of this city in the southwest corner of Georgia were proud of the history of their town.

It was early 1956. John Foster Dulles was the Secretary of State in the second administration of Eisenhower or "Ike", as he was fondly called by many Americans. In those days, the South consistently voted solidly Democratic and was against a Republican administration regardless of who was in Washington. Certain Republicans were disliked more than others, and on the top of the list was John Foster Dulles. Unlike the present, it was always safe in presidential or congressional elections to count on the southern states to vote Democratic. Most people I talked to said their families voted Democratic for generations and that was a carry over from the Civil War when much of the South was burned and devastated by Sherman, one of Lincoln's generals. The hatred of Lincoln's Republican Party was abruptly transferred towards the Democratic party when Lyndon Johnson signed the Civil Rights Act in 1964, that invalidated Jim Crow laws and made segregation illegal, and the National Voting Rights Act in 1965. Since then, the South overwhelmingly supported the Republican Party.

That reminds me of the majority party in Egypt during King Farouk's days, the "Wafd" Party, literally meaning the Delegation Party. It was created in the process of the struggle of the Egyptians against British colonization when a few Egyptian nationalists, some of them rich landlords, formed a delegation headed by Saad Zaghloul to demand independence from the British authorities. When they were arrested, the whole country revolted. That was in 1919 and since that time, and in spite of some splinter movements, the Wafd Party remained the majority party in Egypt. Not a majority of 55%, but an overwhelming majority. There was a popular saying "If the Wafd nominated a stone for election, we would elect it". This blind loyalty or level of commitment was not unlike that of the U.S. South for the Democratic Party. The Wafd symbolized the unity of Egyptians across religious lines and thus included Copts (Egyptian Christians) in the top leadership. They opposed British colonization of Egypt and later opposed the King's corruption and his attempts to defy the Constitution. Being a liberal party, the Wafd was anti-fascist, which was popular in the world those days. When the King flirted with the Axis forces, especially the Nazi regime, the British nearly forced his abdication. Ironically, it is that opposition to fascism that brought the Wafd Party to cooperate with the British during the Second World War, especially when Field Marshal Rommell's Panzer units were already in Egypt near El-Alemain, a coastal city on the Mediterranean. Some Egyptian nationalists were demonstrating in the streets of Cairo and Alexandria shouting "Go forward Rommell!!"

At the time of our visit to Blakely the storm over the Suez Canal was gathering. The British were planning to attack Egypt in collusion with the French and Israelis, presumably in retaliation for the nationalization of the Canal. Secretary of State Dulles initiated this drama when he had the

World Bank withdraw its financial backing of the Aswan High Dam. It was the key project that Nasser championed and was the jewel of his program for the development of Egypt. The High Dam was built south of Aswan to further control the usage of Nile water and to generate electric power to make electricity available for the first time to thousands of Egyptian villages and to provide energy for key industries, such as steel, aluminum and fertilizers. Dulles and the World Bank made Egyptians angry and left Nasser no alternative but to nationalize the Egyptian canal. He decided to generate the funds he needed for the High Dam from the revenues of the Suez Canal that was owned mainly by the British and the French. For generations the Canal was a symbol of foreign domination and injustice. Nasser decided to hit two birds with one stone - get the funds needed for the High Dam, and remove the last ugly symbol of British colonization. He announced the nationalization of the Suez Canal at a rally in Alexandria. The crowd roared in support of an act that restored the dignity of the vast majority of Egyptians. At that specific moment Nasser became a hero of Egypt and the entire Arab World. No Egyptian doubted that the Canal, which was dug by the blood (I say this literally) and sweat of forced Egyptian labor, belonged to Egypt. It was basically robbed from Egypt by the British just as the Rosetta Stone in the British Museum symbolizes the robbery by the colonizers of numerous ancient Egyptian artifacts. Till today, this event evokes such strong feelings of elation and pride as reflected by the immense popularity of a recent Egyptian film "Nasser 56".

On the assigned date, we took a bus from Tallahassee to Blakely. Soheir and I were newlywed and in the midst of the ecstasy and the agony associated with the first few months of marriage. The trip was enjoyable. I always enjoy a bus or a train ride since childhood. In Egypt, I am used to seeing flat fields cultivated with wheat, cotton or vegetables. I never got tired of looking at the various shades of green, golden colors of wheat and white cotton collected by young girls in brightly colored gowns. These colors varied with the season and were punctuated with the color of black earth.

Looking from the window of a Greyhound bus en route to Blakely, the scenes were different, we were fascinated with the reddish color of the soil.

My old slide collection contains numerous photos reflecting this fascination. Photos that display the color of the soil, whenever a highway cut through a hill and exposed the reddish color surrounded by green, a scene which I felt solicited a photo. Arriving at Blakely we were met by a Southern gentleman in his forties wearing a pair of glasses and having a wide smile that revealed his large set of teeth. As I recall his image he looked like Jimmy Carter, the famous U.S. President, or even more like his brother Billy. He drove us in his car after welcoming us and he talked over the phone in his car. That was a first for me. A phone in an automobile - impressive. He talked with his mother, announcing our arrival. As became quite clear later, the mother was clearly the leader of the family. We had to go directly to the Rotary Club meeting where we had a standard light lunch. I gave a speech about the situation in Egypt. My critical statements of Dulles were met by cheers. I was indeed in the solid Democratic South.

The talk went well, with both the audience and the speaker enjoying bashing Dulles, probably for different reasons. The questions reflected the minuscule knowledge of the Club members about Egypt, recent events and U.S. foreign policy. My support of Nasser's actions was unwavering in spite of the fact that my father, a civil engineer and a high-ranking government official, was at the time in political detention for opposing Nasser's monopoly on power. Disagreements on internal issues should never compromise one's position on national issues of paramount importance.

After the luncheon talk, the real fun began. We were driven to the family mansion of our hosts. It was not exactly the mansion of Scarlet in "Gone with the Wind", but it had a touch of similar elegance and tradition. After meeting the mother, we were led to our bedroom upstairs, a lovely room with one of the most comfortable beds I had ever slept in. But what I remember most is the comforter which was light, kept me warm and maybe had ostrich feathers.

After a delicious nap, we woke to a ringing bell, got dressed and went downstairs. The bell aroused our appetite and we were not disappointed. At dinnertime, all the family, mostly sons ranging in age between forty and fifty with their wives, were at the table.

The dining room was elegant with classical furniture and a beautiful chandelier. The family was a warm Southern family, apparently very rich, and we felt very comfortable there. In fact, the mother kind of reminded me with the aunt of my mother who was a powerful woman, very delightful and rich. She was married to a lawyer who was elected repeatedly to the Egyptian Parliament in the Forties, representing the Wafd party. She was not particularly pretty. In fact, she was rather ugly, but most charming and had a powerful presence. When I was a child, I always welcomed the opportunity to visit her large house in Fayoum, an oasis city west of Cairo.

The Blakely dinner was elaborate and it featured quails - simply delicious. The conversation was focused on us, especially my beautiful wife whose English was better than mine with a British accent that seduced most Americans. We talked about Egypt, Alexandria, ancient Egyptians, FSU, our life in the U.S.A. and our families. It was a nice memorable evening. The conversation continued for a while after dinner. When it was bedtime for the mother, we all "had" to retire and to go back to our lovely room.

In the morning, we took a tour of the vast farm that had countless acres of cotton and peanuts. We were shown where they pack the cotton and prepare it for shipment. Over dinner we talked about the history of cotton, how it was spun, woven and dyed in ancient Egypt as well as in India and China. I mentioned how the price of Egyptian cotton, which has the special quality of long strong fibers, increased due to the shortage of exported U.S. cotton during the Civil War when Southern ports were blocked by the North. This development made many farmers rich, and the new fortune made some behave recklessly. That led Viceroy (Khedewi) Ismail to borrow heavily from European financial establishments to finance his ambitious plans to make Egypt "part of Europe". However, Egypt went bankrupt in 1876 after the US Civil War ended and cheap US cotton flooded the market Many farmers lost their fortunes and many dramatic stories were told not unlike those associated with the 1929 U.S. stock market crash. The real drama was the annexation of Egypt by the British which lasted more than seventy years. I remarked that in some strange way Blakely and similar towns in the South were tied partly to Egypt through cotton.

After another fancy dinner, we spent one more night in the elegant bed with the ostrich packed quilt. In the morning we were driven to the bus station. Of course, there were one or two calls from the car phone. It was goodbye and thanks and back to Tallahassee to lectures and examinations, but with lots of appreciation of warm Southern hospitality. When Jimmy Carter was elected U.S. President, I naturally remembered with fondness our short Blakely visit. Blakely bears a strong resemblance to Plains, Georgia, Carter's hometown. However, during our visit we did not see an ugly couch like the one that Jimmy and Billy Carter used to sit on in their gas station in Plains, Georgia.

My maternal grandfather, 1928.

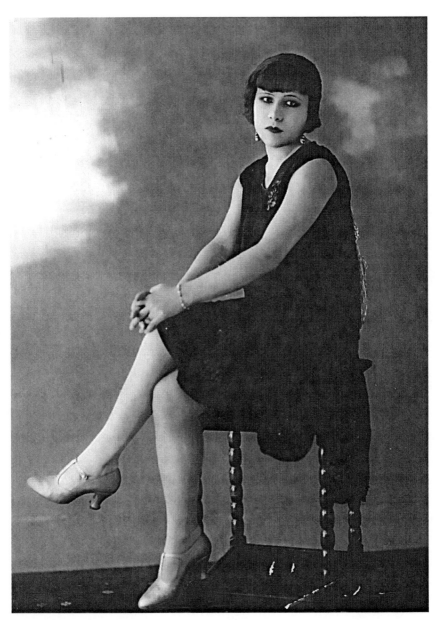

My mother, 1932.

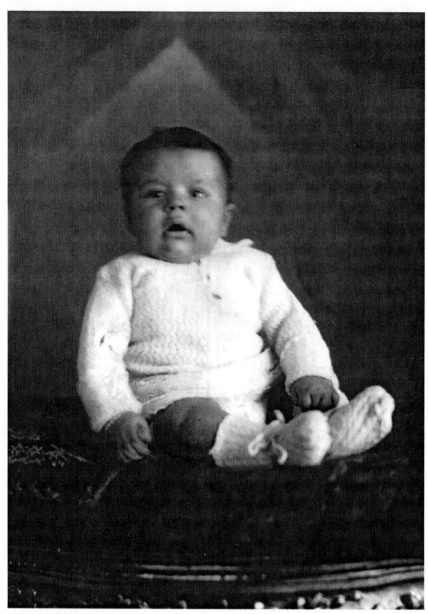

Me as an infant, 1935.

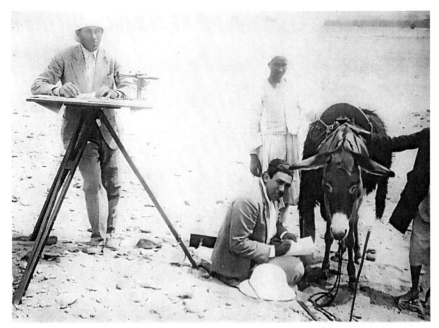

My father on a land survey in Southern Egypt, 1933.

With my Honor's Chemistry colleagues at the Alexandria University Faculty of Science, 1954.

With my friend Ali's Buick, Tallahassee, 1955.

Soheir after our proxy wedding, 1956.

Soheir and I atop the Empire State Building one day after her arrival to the U.S., 1956.

A MANY-SPLENDORED THING—Tallahassee, Sept. 24—Soheir El-Bayoumi, 16-year-old Egyptian bride, recently joined her husband, Mohamed Ashraf El-Bayoumi, at Florida State University.

FSU Student Newspaper Article, 1956.

Bridegroom Was At FSU While His Bride Spoke Vows In Egypt

TALLAHASSEE, Sept. 24.— (Special)—One of Florida State University's prettiest, wittiest, youngest and best qualified freshmen arrived a week ago from Egypt.

Soheir El-Bayoumi, the 16-year-old coed, is a recent bride. She was married Aug. 7 at her home in Alexandria while her bridegroom, Mohamed Ashraf El-Bayoumi, plugged away all day on a research project in a chemistry laboratory at Florida State University. They were married by proxy with his father, Hosney El-Bayoumi, standing in for him.

"That was a day," the 21-year-old husband admitted. "I worked hard, but was happy and had some fun. Whenever anyone interrupted me, I startled him away by explaining I was being married."

BOTH HUSBAND and wife are ambitious. He has been at FSU a year, expects to get a master's degree in biochemistry in January, and then go on for a doctor's degree. He received his BS at Alexandria University and taught there a year before coming to FSU.

The bride lost no time after arrival in enrolling at FSU. During orientation week she took tests which exempted her from a course in English and two in French. She wants to work for a BS in bacteriology, and by going Summer sessions hopes to make it in three years. Back in Egypt she spent two years in an American Mission School, and nine years in a Catholic school under supervision of the British government.

BOTH ARE ISLAMS. Their families have been close neighbors for a number of years in Alexandria. Before the young man left Egypt, he put two rings on his fiancee's right hand, according to their custom. It was only necessary to shift the rings to her left hand at the wedding ceremony.

The ceremony had to take place in Egypt because of the bride's age. She had to be married to get her visa. Exactly a month before her wedding, July 7, she became 16 years old.

Now settled in an apartment near campus at 403 South Copeland, the young couple are keen on everything American. In his year at FSU he has acquired a Southern accent. But she speaks better English with only a slight British accent, and also French fluently. He is beginning to teach her to cook.

FSU Student Newspaper Article, 1956.

Soheir and I in Tallahasee, 1956.

Soheir and I with colleagues at an FSU football game, 1956.

Mrs. Steele with Soheir and I on my FSU Master's in Science graduation day, 1957.

Soheir and I in Killerian Gardens, Tallahassee, 1957.

Soheir and I with neighbors at FSU, 1958.

Soheir and I in our FSU campus apartment, 1958.

Soheir on Broadway, 1958.

Soheir at the English Girls College in Alexandria, Egypt, where she taught, 1963.

EPISODE TWELVE:

Oral Roberts:
Religion, Sex and Dollars

One of the first things that startled me in the USA was to watch Oral Roberts on television doing his thing - healing or, perhaps, fooling people. At first it was a simple tent and hundreds of people attending these shows with Oral Roberts straddling a simple chair. One must admit that there is a hypnotic aspect to the whole thing, not only the magnetic personality of the preacher/healer, but the way the crowd reacted. Even though some of the reaction did not appear genuine and may have been rehearsed, the majority of the audience seemed to believe the performance. After a sick man was healed, the crowd went into a frenzy crying with tears and shouting "Halleluiah!" I had never seen anything like that, except in movies such as "Elmer Gantry," which is a Sinclair Lewis novel that was made into a film co-starring Burt Lancaster and Jean Simmons. Gantry is a charlatan character who uses religion to make money and is a flamboyant man who has abundant sex with women whom he uses to advance his schemes. Oral Roberts' show tops them all. He could heal all illnesses, deafness, paralysis and cancer. All that it took was for him to pray and shout "Heal it in the name of Jesus!", and immediate recovery was assured. Not only that, but some sick television viewers were also healed. While watching from home, they were asked to kneel in front of their TV sets to receive the miraculous healing. Apparently, the healing power was transmitted through radio waves as well.

One is left wondering why there is a need for hospitals or medical facilities and research to combat disease. Why waste billions of dollars when such a healing technique is available? Why is it that when people like Gantry are exposed as frauds their practices are never discredited permanently? How come they were able to recover like a cat with nine lives, or is it that their healing power extends to resurrection from scandals? Why is it that those obviously intelligent charismatic evangelists are often mixed up in financial and sex scandals? Apparently such a cocktail of sex, drugs, religion, wealth and sometimes politics is common to famous preachers of all religions. I recall Mr. Braikaa in Alexandria, Egypt in the early 1980s who concocted a similar mixture for his believers. Among other things, he would require female members to kiss him twenty one times on his lips and male members would measure the length of their penises. However, the group was eventually arrested and several members got jail sentences.

In a general sense, the Oral Roberts phenomenon was not completely new to me. Even though some may not admit it, it is true that in Egypt, among Muslims and Christians alike, the majority believe in magic, holy people who can heal, charms that protect from envy, and relieving individuals from supernatural beings called "jinn" (or genies) who cause a variety of harm, particularly impotence to men and untold havoc to women, including marrying them and making them pregnant! There are individuals who claim that they control "jin", to uncover crimes and find stolen items and kidnapped or lost children and cause "jin" to perform important errands and services.

In many Egyptian communities, some are considered "blessed". Often, they are mentally retarded poor individuals who can do good deeds in return for a donation in the form of food or clothing. Our rather rich neighbors who had a son who kept failing the high school diploma resorted to some of those people to no avail. I know some cases where married women who were desperate to become pregnant, others concerned that their husbands are planning to get a second wife and women desperate to get married tried holy men or women. The success rate was meager. When a married person is having an extra-marital affair, services were offered to make the man impotent specifically to women other than his wife. Services to do the opposite were also offered. Newly married men with potency problems were often told that a "jinneya", a female jinn, loves him or is married to him, and was the cause of the problem. A relic was provided with instructions for when and where to throw it, usually in a canal where the jinneya resides. Since the problem is usually psychological, believers were often cured. Protective charms of various types are used, mainly a copy of the Koran, as a device to protect from envy, spirits, "jinn", as well as accidents. That explains the copy of Koran in most taxicabs in Egypt today, like St. Christopher's image for Christians. There is no evidence to date that such devices lowered accident rates. However, most people feel comfortable exercising the habit. Often, a "hejab" is prescribed by special people for a fee. Certain rituals and deeds are associated with providing the "hejab", which is often a folded or sealed written prayer in Arabic or an unknown language, sometimes hieroglyphic symbols. A "hejab" should never be opened individuals are warned, or else the "jinn"or some mysterious force will cause untold harm. It should be put under a pillow or pinned on one's undershirt. In fact, I once shared a room with an Indian professor when we both were attending a conference and he had not one but several hejabs (or what is equivalent to it) hanging over his undershirt. What makes this particularly interesting is that he was a scientist who presumably was using scientific methodology.

Mass hysteria associated with religion occurs everywhere in the world and does not spare any religion. When I was a freshman in college I witnessed an example of this. I went with my uncle to the "moolid", the celebration of the birthday of one of the holy men. The train we took only had standing room in one of the train cargo carriages. When we arrived, we found the city very crowded. The main feature of the celebration was the procession led by the descendent of the holy man, or "Khaleefa", who rides an ornamented horse while wearing special garb, including a heavy head dress that presumably belonged to the late holy man. My uncle and I were guests and thus we had the honor of being close to the horse. We were encircled by police who were preventing waves of people from trying to touch the "Khalifa" in order to be blessed, healed or have their wishes granted. Donations in cash and gold were deposited in a special box located and guarded at the shrine of the holy man in an impressive mosque. Well, the procession continued and the heat did not quell the crowd's excitement. In the midst of all this, I noticed a very bad smell and mistakenly thought that it was the horse manure. The horse was innocent. It was the "Khaleefa" who apparently had diarrhea, and the smell was unbearable. In the mean time the crowds kept pushing, attempting to touch the holy man or those near him. Even though Islam does not recognize holy men with special powers, these beliefs thrive and are popular.

Oral Roberts, however, was something else. The large audience, the theatrics involved, and, more importantly, the instant healing of so many diseases. A person in apparent need of healing is asked to come forward and is often helped to come forward because of his or her hopeless health situation. An assistant would stand immediately behind the patient and the healer explains the patient's dire situation, prays and then touches the patient's forehead and shouts "Heal it!". The patient falls back into the arms of the assistant and then the patient is miraculously cured. The disease, regardless of its nature, vanishes just like that and the patient jumps around with intense joy. A paralyzed leg suddenly is bursting with energy, a blind person's vision is restored, and a deaf person can instantly "hear an ant crawling" as we say in Egypt. The reaction of the audience, who are now in the thousands, is wild. Several go into a frenzy. Regardless, several, if not most, of those "miraculous" healings have been proven to be fraudulent.

One great "miracle" that topped all was that Mr. Roberts became very rich. In later years these shows became more elaborate as the money continued to pour in. I was fascinated by watching these shows and was particularly flabbergasted one day when Oral Roberts announced that Jesus will recall him if he does not raise several millions dollars by a specified date. He appealed to the audience to give their money so that he wouldn't die. He raised more than he asked for. I was surprised by the number of people that responded and by the audacity of Mr. Roberts.

One question lingered in my mind: why Mr. Roberts, with the assurance of being welcomed in heaven, was so reluctant to leave this material life to the point where he was crying on television?

Roberts went further than most by establishing a University in Tulsa,

Oklahoma obeying a direct order from God! Another order followed from Jesus to build a hospital merging faith and medicine and commissioned Roberts to find a cure for cancer. The hospital lost millions and closed after eight years.

Oral Roberts was not alone. I saw other evangelists perform on TV. Prominent among them was none other than Jimmy Swaggart. He proclaimed his mission to be the eradication of filth from the face of the planet. He targeted heavy metal music and pornographic publications such as Hustler and Playboy magazines. When the scandal of being caught watching a female prostitute performing sexual acts for his lusty eyes, Swaggart was not deterred. Instead, he told his flock that the Lord advised him that it was none of their business. Although his credibility sank, it later recovered. His exposure was the result of a war waged among evangelists competing for a bigger share of the TV market.

Another remarkable TV show was that of Jim Baker and his wife, Tammy Faye, who sang for the worshippers. Jim and Tammy specialized in a Disney-like religion. Building resort compounds with swimming pools for their flock to love one another and enjoy luxuries. Scandal followed. It involved the usual cocktail: sex, money and swindling their flock.

Some may regard my comments as being disrespectful to religions. On the contrary, I simply consider the practice of using religion to fool people as the mother of all insults. Watching shows which propagate such deception, one can not escape the impression that they are like other TV entertainment shows, complete with advertisements such as the toothpaste that will brighten your teeth and make you an instant Don Juan or a concoction like Geritol that brings immediate strength.

Televangelism is a unique American production, and fits the impression of "Amreeka The Wonder Land" that I carried with me when I first arrived in the US. There are signs, however, that a similar phenomenon is spreading and is becoming global as several satellite channels in the Arab World proves. Shows ranging from dream interpretations, religious preaching and advice to the use of supernatural devices are striving to join the elite members of the Praise the Lord Club.

EPISODE THIRTEEN:

"You Folks Like Pineapple, Don't You?"

I do not remember ever laughing as much as I did that night. We had invited an Egyptian couple for dinner in our small apartment, which was walking distance from campus. He was a young professor of mathematics who was quite a jovial fellow. His interesting wife came from a respected intellectual family. Somehow the timing was perfect and the chemistry was just right. I do not even recall what made us laugh. It is interesting how sometimes one remembers moments of intense emotions such as laughter or anger and yet forgets the causes.

Now I remember one episode concerning an Egyptian fellow who had just arrived from Egypt. He was desperately trying to be Americanized instantly, so he decided to buy a pair of shorts and he wrongly bought "hot pants", a woman's style that was too short and zipped from the side. He paraded the shorts with great pride and could not understand why it caused such wild laughter. That does not sound particularly funny now, and maybe it was not funny even then, but we kept laughing like *hashasheen* (hash smokers) even though we had neither hasheesh nor alcohol. In Egypt it is said that people who smoke hasheesh laugh wildly and joke perpetually. As a matter of fact, I suspect that highly creative Egyptian jokes were born in hasheesh gatherings. These jokes become popular quickly, particularly the clever ones. They deal with a variety of topics ranging from sex to politics and often expose ironies and contradictions, personal and societal.

Hasheesh is the Arabic word for hemp, a potent type of marijuana, which is widely used in the States, but is illegal. Smoking it was the subject of presidential election politics, whether you inhale it or not! It is interesting to note that the word assassin is derived from the word "hashasheen". The reason assassins are associated with hasheesh is a bit of history and a lot of myth. The legend revolves around a mysterious character, Hassan Al-Sabbah born in Qom, in today's Iran, who was a Twelfth Century compatriot of Omar Al-Khayyam of "Rubaiyaat" fame. Qom is better known for being the seat of Iranian mullahs who rule Iran today. Al-Sabbah, as the story goes, led a group of men who were blindly obedient to him to the point of being willing to kill without hesitation once he ordered them to do so. Indeed, upon his orders they carried out several assassinations of his foes across what is now the Middle East. To obtain their total obedience, he promised paradise not only in the afterlife but in the present life. He rewarded those who succeeded at various phases of obedient training with hasheesh. The training was described as being extremely harsh and tedious, sort of like Marine or Navy Seal training. When they became euphoric after having hasheesh, he led them to his magnificent garden with fruit trees and running canals, a sort of a paradise, particularly for a desert environment. In some versions of the story they had sex with young women, sort of the equivalent of "Hoor Elein", beautiful virgin women that are one of the rewards to those Muslims who go to paradise. No wonder they competed to carry Al-Sabbah's orders with zeal and without fear of death, for death will grant them eternal life in the real paradise. The word "assassin" was thus born. Most probably, however, the legend was based on false or exaggerated stories propagated in Europe by some of the returning Crusaders. In Egypt, the term hashash could mean a real smoker of hasheesh, but more often it means a jovial person who loves to laugh a lot. Regardless, the term has no remote relation to assassinations.

Charismatic personalities that use their power of influence, drugs and sex to control vulnerable young people to the point of having them kill others when a command is given borders on madness and arises in different societies from time to time. Charles Manson mesmerized several young Americans by songs, sex orgies and LSD trips. He threw into the cocktail mixture a bit of politics as well as claims of being a Christ and a Devil at the same time. Obedient disciples, or should I say "assassins", blindly obeyed their guru and killed for him. From everywhere there are ample cases showing the phenomenon cutting across boundaries of culture or time. This does not make it less appalling or frightening.

We kept talking and laughing with our Egyptian guests until well after midnight. One hour or so afterwards, I suddenly felt a very sharp pain in my right lower abdomen. I immediately thought of the appendix. My wife did not know how to drive at that time, but after that night learning to drive became a top priority for her. I had to roll over the carpeted steps and to drive my car. My body took a most unusual posture to minimize the pain. If some other driver, or worse, the police would have seen me, they surely would have concluded that I was dead drunk. I was drunk all right - with unbearable pain. I managed somehow to arrive to Tallahassee Memorial Hospital for which I have a particular affinity - my first daughter, Gigi, was later born there. I asked for my doctor, an old gentleman, who arrived shortly. After a brief examination, he suggested to take Milk of Magnesia. He thought that the problem was kidney related, since the sharp pain was on my right side. I politely refused to take any laxative. I was convinced that the cause of the pain was the appendix. My physician asked me if I would like to see a surgeon, I immediately replied with affirmation. After a very brief examination by the surgeon who came promptly, I was taken to surgery immediately. This demonstrated the importance of patient participation with the doctor to reach a correct diagnosis. It was the appendix all right, and somehow it acted up after an unusual dose of laughter. In common Egyptian wisdom, excessive laughter is bad or even sinful. In fact, some believe that if you laugh a lot, you will be saddened later by some event and they may even utter a prayer to lighten or even eliminate the negative consequences of laughter. Some would say "allahoma egaalo kheir", meaning "God please make things all right". This theory of balance in sadness and pleasures or good and bad news or happiness and misery is one of those unquestioned inherited beliefs. It is sort of a law of balance or conservation of emotions, falsely mimicking the law of conservation of energy. This logic may confirm that my predicament was clear proof of the law.

There had been a pause in my awareness when I found myself in a hospital room. I must have had the operation already! I was drowsy, but I could occasionally hear the nurses talk, then I heard them giggling while handling my penis. From time to time a nurse would ask me if I would like to take a pain killer. Pain killers kill the pain all right, but there was no pill to kill the effects of the pain killer, which left me in an awkward state. The following morning, a nurse approached my bed. She was speaking with a heavy Southern accent. I knew then the stigma attached to Southern women whose drawls make them seem stupid in the eyes of Yankees. By now, I had lived in the South for a few years and I had, and still have, a very warm feeling and great affection for several aspects of Southern culture in spite of my revulsion at the racist attitude that outwardly prevailed at that time. This nurse asked about my preference of breakfast, including my choice of eggs ("sunny sad uup, scraaaambled, with greets or not"). When she asked about the type of juice I would prefer, I chose pineapple juice. Being in Florida, I had plenty of orange juice, so I wanted to drink something different. In Egypt, we called pineapple "ananass" and I loved it as a child and I still do. No pineapple trees are grown in Egypt, but canned slices dipped in delicious syrup were imported. My mother bought a few large cans every time she visited the family's old Greek grocer in Cairo. We even gave the grocer the nickname "Ananass".

When I asked for pineapple juice, the nurse responded, "You folks like pineapple don't you?". I asked, "What do you mean "You folks? To which folks do I belong?". Well, she became utterly confused. I don't know if she assumed that I am a foreign Negro. I was, and remain, extremely proud of being both Egyptian and African. By that time my initial resentment of being associated with "Negroes" had disappeared, but my anger and revulsion at racism was enhanced. I must say I developed a feeling of sorrow for the ignorance of those who felt superior because they were white. The nurse gave me a long empty gaze. When I looked straight into her eyes, I began a long journey into an infinite void. My journey was interrupted when she said, "Where are you from?". I answered, "I am from Egypt", but the gaze continued. "Do you know where Egypt is?," I asked. She did not respond. I tried to help her by saying, "Egypt is where the Great Pyramids are, also the Sphinx and the Nile". She said, "Oh yeah, somewhere in the Pacific. It must be near Hawaii". For a few seconds I imagined hula-hula dancers wiggling their beautiful naked breasts and bodies in the shadow of the Great Pyramids and under the watchful eyes of the Sphinx. I finally said "Yes, we folk like pineapple don't we".

I found it incredible how in the US knowledge of foreign lands and cultures is blurred at best or more likely non existent. Such is the breeding ground for racism and ethnic prejudice that can be transformed by ambitious individuals into violent expressions. The sad thing is that lack of knowledge often extends to one's own country manifested by an inability to locate major cities or identify important present day, not to mention historical, personalities.

EPISODE FOURTEEN:

Mrs. Steel

It was a comfortable arrangement. We were newly married, short on money, and my wife did not particularly like being alone at night when I was in the laboratory late conducting experiments. So we shared an apartment with an old American lady, Mrs. Steel. The apartment was one of several owned by a Syrian couple, Mitch and Rose. We knew about the desire of Mrs. Steel to share her apartment from one of our Egyptian friends who previously lived in the premises when I first arrived to the US.

We had a room for ourselves and shared the living room and the kitchen with Mrs. Steel who instantly liked my wife and called her "my baby". Mrs. Steel had a very coarse voice. It took us a few weeks to get used to it and to recognize her true kindness and tenderness contrary to what her name may have indicated. In the late evening, we often watched television with Mrs. Steel, and at supper time we watched the news together. I still remember Willie the Weatherman and the children's show that preceded the news. The host wore a cowboy outfit and called the kids "buckaroos". It was presidential campaign time also. Eisenhower and Nixon were running against Stevenson and Kefaver. My knowledge about American politics was limited then, but I already became interested in presidential campaigns as well as the races for Florida Governor and Senate. I attended a democratic vice-presidential rally where Senator Estes Kefauver spoke and I liked his stands against inequalities in wealth and power, as well as corruption and organized crime.

I remember Governor Collins, a well-liked man in Florida who was also interested in foreign students. In this capacity we had the occasion to meet him. I remember how I was impressed to see him crossing a street in downtown Tallahassee with two companions and how he waited for the traffic light to change. There were no guards, no formalities. Utter simplicity in contrast to today's besieged leaders who can not take a step without guards and secret police. Such simplicity was quite a contrast to the usual embroidered honorific behavior we are unfortunately accustomed to in Egypt and perhaps most of the third world and monarchies like England. Several years later I was a witness to a bizarre example of honorific behavior. I was attending a science conference in Abuja, Nigeria when we were invited to attend a speech by President Sani Abacha. The speech was preceded by music played by a very colorful band. It was amusing that after each segment of the President's speech the band would give a short musical interlude, mainly drums followed by a cymbals finale, similar to what happens when Tonight Show hosts finish a joke or a remark that is accented by the music. I was not prepared for this, so I burst out laughing when it was done the first time. Some officials noticed, but I did not particularly care since I had little respect for President Abacha for his violation of human rights in Nigeria.

In the evening we engaged in conversation with Mrs. Steel about Egypt and casual matters, but our exchanges were dominated by the television, which he had on most of the time till midnight and beyond. There was no cable at that time. TV was black and white and the number of channels were limited. In fact, Channel Six was the only available channel with clear reception, which was a blessing in disguise. The habit of flipping channels was not known yet, neither was the competition for who would have the remote control. It is interesting how new technologies, including minor ones, affect and even alter our social habits and interactions. So egalitarian and simple TV etiquette gave way to arguments about who holds the new symbol of familial power - the TV remote. Gone are the days when watching TV involved a simple switching on and an occasional adjustment of the volume or the rabbit ears antenna.

We watched "Amos & Andy", old movies (that were not so old then), quiz shows and, of course, hundreds of those notorious commercials. Because Mrs.

Steel did not like Dinah Shore, every time she appeared on the screen, and that was often, she made a negative comment. Dinah Shore would appear in a fancy Chevrolet singing "See the USA in your Chevrolet". I personally liked the commercial, but after several times it was exhausting. Mrs. Steel did like a young man who appeared with a tweed jacket and lustrous hair as the host of General Electric Theater. The name of that man was Ronald Reagan who later became the President of the USA for eight years. Only in the USA could an actor become the President of the country deciding the fate of the American people, if not the whole world, including the potential launching of a global nuclear war. Later I came to realize that strategic decisions, while in principle are made by the President, have important inputs by several institutions and individuals and it is seldom or never a one-person decision even if it appears otherwise. The GE slogan was "Progress is our Most Important Product". We saw many elegant major and small appliances. Very impressive, but at the time we had no thoughts of acquiring any of them. Reagan was no doubt a charming and effective salesman. We quickly learned the statement that "What is Good for the General is Good for the USA". It took many years to fully understand the implications of such profound slogans.

The TV shows that we regularly watched and enjoyed were many including: "Lassie", "Father Knows Best", "What's My Line?", The Steve Allen Show and, of course, The Ed Sullivan Show. It feels now that these shows were far more interesting than the current ones. Either we are frozen in time and affected by the good old time syndrome or our feeling reflects reality. One hilarious show that attracted our attention was "Amos and Andy". The characters were most amusing, naïve Amos who always was easy to exploit, and Andy who displayed an unjustified sense of confidence and last, but definitely not least, the sly King Fish. Every week their episodes brought intense laughter. That sitcom later caused some controversy as to stereotyping Blacks and because of some racially offensive depictions. At the time, I was not conscious of these issues and considered the show to be an interesting comedy just like another exciting comedy show, "I Love Lucy".

Mrs. Steel was fond of watching TV commercials. Unfortunately, she believed all the claims made by the advertisements. She would order kitchen gadgets that appeared impressive and able to perform marvels on TV, but often proved impractical. Mrs. Steel was not rich and was obviously living off modest means so I felt sorry for her wasting her precious dollars. On the other hand, she must have had some pleasure in imagining being a modern cook using new gadgets or fantasizing about having a youthful look. Thus, when a commercial claiming that a magical cream would tighten the facial skin would come on, she would scribble the phone number and a few minutes later she would call and order COD. No credit cards or charging via phones was yet available. After trying the cream for weeks no effect was visible as her skin remained wrinkled. Frankly, I find a certain beauty in wrinkled faces of old people. Also, facial lines on middle aged individuals reflect personalities. A jovial person who smiled frequently for many years would have lines printed permanently on their face, particularly around the eyes. Likewise, kindness, worry, meanness and anger show on facial expressions after many years. One could say that the Dorian Gray myth is real in some way. Some well-known politicians have a sneering look and facial expressions that reveal a conniving, calculating personality. Learning to read facial characteristics and body language in general can be quite useful, as well as amusing.

Our neighbor, Mitch, would come over sometimes to watch television. At the end of the broadcast, the National Anthem was played and Mrs. Steel would stand up and salute the waving flag on TV, and if Mitch, who had recently become a US citizen, was around, she would scold him for not standing up. Eventually he would stand up, but no salutes. She would say that we did not have to stand up since we were not citizens. Mitch would argue sometimes that he was not yet sworn in as a citizen, but when he was sworn in he had no excuse and always stood up. It was amusing to see adults doing that, although that was not void of symbolism. What added to our amusement is that Mrs. Steel had an old parrot that she often had perched on her left shoulder. She would say that he was also saluting Old Glory with her when she stood up. I politely gestured agreement when she insisted that this was the case. Being a Southerner, she had preferred to salute the Confederate flag as many Southerners did those days, but reality imposed itself. She spoke fondly of General Robert E. Lee, calling him her favorite General. It was easy to admire Lee's brilliance and chivalry.

We also watched mysteries and horror movies with Mrs. Steel. One night, we watched more than the usual share of horror episodes. In particular, there was a movie that was especially frightening. I forgot the name of the movie, but after we were relaxed when the bad guy was killed after a long, horrific struggle, we were all shocked when the bad guy suddenly rose again and attempted to kill the innocent victim. That was more than enough. It was like "Cape Fear". Nowadays, one expects as a standard trick that the bad guy, and sometimes now a bad woman to ensure gender equality, would rise unexpectedly at least once to strike again. Although we have now developed immunity against this trick after it became common, at the time neither Mrs. Steel nor I had such immunity. Soheir did not need any since she never watched violent or horror movies. After saying good night to Mrs. Steel, I went to bed, and found Soheir fast asleep. Although we started the morning as usual, we sensed something unusual, perhaps that it was too quiet. Also, I was surprised that Mrs. Steel was not up yet. I peeked into Mrs. Steel's room and was startled to see her lying on her back with her eyes wide open gazing towards the ceiling. I screamed, "Mrs. Steel is dead!!". Soheir started to cry profusely and I was profoundly sad, but my eyes were dry. I ran to our neighbor Mitch and his wife, who also became sad. They immediately called to inform Mrs. Steel's relatives. I am convinced that Mrs. Steel was a TV casualty, the poor lady was shocked to death by the stupid horror movie.

When her family came at midday, I witnessed a scene which reminds me now with a scene straight from "Zorba the Greek". I would not be exaggerating when I say that it seems as if the director of the movie plagiarized that scene with Mrs. Steel's name changed into Bobolina. The family descended like vultures and began snatching the belongings of Mrs. Steel. Including her parrot who must had been saddened as we were by the whole ugly looting scene. In the midst of all this an occasional expression of sorrow was displayed when etiquette demanded. We were disgusted, but could not kick them out as Zorba did in the film and we became more sad and depressed.

In a few days, as soon as we found another available apartment, we moved out. The image of Mrs. Steel standing up saluting Old Glory with her parrot standing on her left shoulder remained a living memory for me. As we were leaving the apartment for the last time, I said with tears in my eyes "Goodbye dear Mrs. Steel" and in a very coarse voice like Mrs. Steel's I said to my wife, "Let us go my baby".

EPISODE FIFTEEN:

Going to Hell

Our life as a couple in Tallahassee took the flavor of a gypsy life. We moved often from one place to another as our priorities changed. A desire to live within the budget compelled us sometimes to share a regular apartment with an old woman. However, a strong desire to live comfortably led us to seek living in an air-conditioned apartment, a luxury at that time. These swings in priorities prompted us to venture and to try unorthodox ways. Some say we were ahead of our time. My wife and I decided to share an apartment with an Italian post-doctoral and his wife. Many of our friends raised eyebrows and a few had their own fantasies of imaginary sexual orgies and wife-swapping. Sharing allowed us to have an air-conditioned apartment at an acceptable cost, which was terrific. Tallahassee's heat and humidity lied outside the confines of the apartment. Walking briefly to the air-conditioned lab was a good reminder of the luxury of living in an air-conditioned apartment. It worked very well and we managed to protect most of our privacy. There were added bonuses, one being the added security for my young wife when I was working late in the lab. The arrangement also gave my wife the opportunity to learn a few Italian dishes which delighted our tastes for a while before they disappeared from our menu. Unfortunately, the couple moved to California and we had to look for a new place. We couldn't afford the rent, but we were spoiled so we looked for another air-conditioned place. We found an apartment close to campus, air-conditioned but rather small. The apartment was one of twelve apartments or so built in a grove surrounded by many trees, which gave us the illusion of living in a mini tropical jungle especially when it rained as it often did.

The apartments belonged to an English teacher on campus in her fifties. Her husband, Mr. Leslie, was in his sixties. I remember his artificial teeth that he clicked continuously with his tongue when he spoke. These apartments looked like a nice setting for a television series not unlike "Melrose Place", though more conservative. Several young couples lived in the compound. We particularly liked a couple, Johnny and Anne. They were a friendly, compatible couple. They loved each other and it was always enjoyable to be with them and go on picnics with them when our time allowed it. Another couple, who lived below them, was Martha Ann and her husband Billy. Billy had a fancy Chevrolet that he was obsessed with, always polishing it and putting additional gadgets in it. He was a spoiled, immature person who didn't do well in school, barely passing when he passed a course and always flunking a few. Martha Ann was ambitious and bright, but had a mean streak in her personality. She was his high school sweetheart, but I got the impression that she didn't really love him and certainly didn't respect him. It seems her marriage was, partly at least, an opportunistic exercise for her. He was rich and she had a flashy beauty, was flirtatious and displayed her body rather liberally even in those days. She took some chemistry courses and I remember seeing her one weekend in the analytical chemistry lab making up an experiment involving titration while wearing a flashy, shining swimming suit. A young Italian post-doctoral helped her very enthusiastically. I thought to myself, that is how titration experiments should be conducted! In a few months, Billy was gone as Martha Ann divorced him and her name was changed to become Miss Colombini.

Almost every week we met at Mrs. Leslie's apartment for coffee and dessert, it was always a nice gathering. Mr. and Mrs. Leslie were not particularly intelligent individuals, but at least Mrs. Leslie knew some English literature. Mr. Leslie's knowledge about anything was dismal. I believe he had very limited education.

One day, Johnny told us a secret. Mr. Leslie likes me very much, but he is agonizing over the fact that I am going straight to hell. Nevertheless, since he liked me, he was dedicated to saving my soul. My inner thoughts reminded me how the slogan of "saving souls" had led to forcibly displacing thousands. The pioneers had their share of liberating the souls of hundreds of thousands of Native Americans. He wanted to accompany me to church and have me meet his minister. I immediately said that I do not mind at all to go to church as it would be an interesting experience. So Johnny relayed this terrific news to Mr. Leslie and he was delighted. We agreed to go the next Sunday to his Methodist church. I tried to explain to Mr. Leslie that Moslems also believe in Jesus as well as other prophets. For him that was not enough, the issue is not believing, but how you believe. I had to believe that Jesus is the sole savior, with emphasis on sole. It mattered to him not only that I belong to a church and practice the various rituals, but also which church. Thus, he would not be pleased if I decided to be Catholic. However, he exhibited some flexibility as to which Protestant denomination I would belong to with a clear preference for the Methodist church. When I came to the US, I was totally surprised at the differences between various sects of Christianity, and to discover the extent of polarization that existed. This clearly manifested itself later when many voters opposed Jack Kennedy for US President just because he was Catholic, but, to the credit of those Protestants that supported him, he was elected.

When I delayed fulfilling my commitment for reasons related to my studies, Mr. Leslie thought I had reneged or that I was not serious in the first place. He was, therefore, surprised when I told him that I was available to go with him to the church that Sunday. Together we went to attend the service. The message of the minister was quite good. He talked about loving thy neighbor, which was befitting since my neighbor was accompanying me, and thus we were practicing the minister's advice. Mr. Leslie introduced me to the minister. We shook hands and exchanged a few pleasant words. I truly have deep respect for all religions, but I had no interest or desire to convert to another religion. As a matter of fact, I used to enjoy hearing church bells ringing a nice tune on Sunday mornings. Moreover, I was troubled by the obvious hypocrisy of not allowing Blacks in the church and not allowing them to be neighbors in the first place. When I raised these questions with Mr.

Leslie he was clearly annoyed and later became visibly angry. He emphasized repeatedly that he does not hate Blacks and believed that they must be treated kindly. However, they must live separately from Whites. Obviously, he treated Soheir and I as White, or Caucasians as our visa identified us. Otherwise, we would not have been allowed to rent one of their apartments. He noted God's wisdom in creating mankind in different colors, and rationalized that segregation was valid because if God meant us to be equal, He would have created us in one color. Such pseudo logic camouflaged in a religious wrapping had always amused me. A similar case was used decades ago stating that if God wanted us to fly, He would have created us with wings. Of course we have creative minds that provided us with huge flying objects called airplanes! I must say, however, that Mr. Leslie must have liked us in a sincere way to the point of wishing that we would belong to the same faith.

We did not see Mr. Leslie for several days. Later Johnny and Ann told us he was sad that he could not save me. I really did not know exactly what Mr. Leslie expected after our church visit. Perhaps he envisioned a miracle like the ones we saw on televangelist shows, suddenly seeing the light shouting "Halleluiah" since that did not happen. Mr. Leslie's verdict must have been that I was indeed going to hell. He did not mention Soheir so it was not clear if she would join me or not. Perhaps she was protected because she attended a Catholic school in Alexandria.

EPISODE SIXTEEN:

Colored Edition: Read All About It!

One afternoon, I got a telephone call from the Foreign Student Advisor asking Soheir and I to participate in a United Nations Day activity. The activity involved visiting a "Negro" elementary school in Tallahassee. We accepted of course.

For many Third World people the UN is a world body that has asymmetric power relations since the victors in the Second World War each have a veto power in the most important council, the Security Council. Therefore, the UN cannot be neutral in many important issues, although UN agencies are doing good work in the area of health and cultural preservation and monitoring peace agreements when that occurs. For us, some of the memorable scenes and figures during the Fifties included Count Bernadotte, Krishna Menon and the Khrushchev scene of him banging his shoe on the table quickly joined by his Foreign Minister Andree Gromyko. Of particular significance for us, were the visits of Nasser and Castro to the UN in New York, which also included visits to Harlem.

We both gave short speeches regarding Egypt and world peace. The class seemed to have enjoyed our visit. It was not every day that they meet Egyptians! They were particularly elated that we were from Africa and our talk about pharaohs, the pyramids, the Nile and Africa excited them. Someone took some photos of us talking to two of the young kids. We returned quickly to our routine of attending classes, going to the library, studying and, for me, preparing for experiments in the laboratory.

On the weekend, I received a phone call from the local newspaper, The Tallahassee Democrat, which I read regularly since it was the only available newspaper. At the time, newspapers like The New York Times were not available except at the library on a delayed basis. The caller mentioned that my photo with the kids and Soheir appeared in the paper. I expressed my surprise for I had not seen it, thinking that I perhaps missed it. The caller informed me that our photo was published in the "Colored Edition". I exclaimed, "How come I do not get the Colored Edition and why have I not ever seen a Colored Edition?" He answered, "I do not know, but if you want to see your photo you can come to the Tallahassee Democrat office downtown". I told him I would. Downtown Tallahassee was walking distance from campus, so it was not a big deal walking. Besides, we did not have a car then.

When I walked into the Tallahassee Democrat office I was more curious to see the newspaper in color, and to learn why I did not get it regularly instead of the black and white version! I was led to a large room and was told, "Here is today's Colored Edition." The paper was not in color. It was black and white, and my sluggish computer started to click as I flipped the paper. It was the same version as the regular edition with one exception: the social page was exclusively for the Negro community with news of birthdays of black kids, weddings for blacks and obituaries for black souls.

How stupid of me. After almost two years in the community living in the land of "Separate but Equal," I did not realize that this extended to newspapers. I still did not get that the word "Colored" primarily meant "Negro" and not the colors of the spectrum!

EPISODE SEVENTEEN:
Eat, Drink and Gossip at Mecca: Daily Pilgrimage

The coffee break was an additional new concept for me and a welcomed one. It became a way to escape from work, a chance to rejuvenate and a delightful opportunity to socialize and gossip. It was all those things but it had nothing to do with sipping coffee. I did not drink coffee at that time; instead I enjoyed having a banana split which I thought is a great invention. In Egypt, I often had a delicious ice cream cone in Gleem, an upscale district of Alexandria. I did not worry about the haunting calories. Quite the contrary. I was underweight, so I indulged in having splits without any guilt.

Banana splits reminded me of an invention by a cheerful Egyptian professor friend of mine whose last name was amusing: "father of turbans" or in Arabic abo-elamayem. He often stopped his small Austin car and bought hot sweet potato from a street vendor, an act which some frowned upon and considered it unbecoming for a university professor. I admired this aspect of his personality: being himself. I resent contrived formalities and appreciate spontaneity. We would then go to a fancy café (Delice) by the corniche, which served delicious ice cream in special glass cups. He would put the hot sweet potato on a plate and add ice cream scoops. His short lived joy was evident. This treat was followed by another deadly one, smoking a cigarette while sipping Turkish coffee. He would hold the smoke while swallowing some coffee and then at last release the smoke with great pleasure as if he were experiencing a sexual climax. Unfortunately, this habit killed him prematurely.

The banana split was more sophisticated than his invention with three flavors and different toppings on each scoop, covered with nuts and whipped cream and in the middle a bright red cherry on the top. The entire assembly was served in a boat like dish. It was fun choosing the order of gulping the different flavors and enjoying the toppings. I learned much later that the banana split was invented by a pharmacist named David Strickler in Latrobe, Pennsylvania and quickly became popular.

Coffee breaks soon became a regular practice specially that Mecca was close to the Chemistry Department where I spent most of my time. The daily ritual was never boring because each time the company was not the same. I met different people, students studying different subjects as well as professors from Chemistry and other departments. It was certainly very different from the annual religious pilgrimage ritual in Mecca. Being an Egyptian was kind of a novelty on campus. Few had ever met an Egyptian. Some would greet me in a Hollywood movie style which was amusing because it did not bear any resemblance to the way we greet each other on the streets of Cairo or Alexandria. We usually gesture a salute with one hand silently or with an expression like "saida" literally meaning happiness or "salam alaikom" meaning peace unto you.

Ice cream was not my only popular item at Mecca, sometimes it was preceded by a delicious turkey sandwich. An authentic turkey sandwich, meaning slices of a real roasted turkey unlike in taste and texture to the "processed" turkey roll we see these days. At the beginning, it was confusing to answer questions regarding my choice of dressing for the salad because I simply did not know any of the choices available, so I randomly tried several until I settled on a favorite one or two.

Ordering a hamburger required knowing the answer to a few questions: How do you like it? What do you like on it? Do you want cheese with it? At the time there was only one kind, American cheese so I was spared one more question. One had to answer quickly because there were others waiting in line. My accent did not help either. Before the yellow arches and the Big Mac moved in, hamburgers were made of genuine beef and were more delicious and healthier.

Aside from the fun and the refreshing effect of such interludes, there was another hidden useful and unplanned aspect to Mecca's coffee breaks. Somehow when you are out of the usual medium, one's thoughts are different and perhaps clearer. It just happened that one of the molecular models which turned out to be ideal for my studies was conceived during a coffee break with my friend. Not only that, it later led to a nice discovery of a new phenomenon: "double proton transfer" that occurs in the excited state of the molecular system. I sat one time with my colleague, Strickler (no relation to the inventor of the banana split, as far as I know). Together we asked the question what is the simplest possible system that has the perfect features to study given our knowledge of the theory and its requirement. We drew the molecular formula of such an ideal system on a napkin. We did not know whether such a substance was synthesized before or not. In the library I found that it was, so I immediately embarked on preparing it and after I succeeded I found that some company sells the material in pure form so I took it from there. My colleague, who became the chemistry department chairman in one of universities in Colorado, was happy that he shared with me such a finding. It all began in Mecca.

It was erroneously claimed that a much bigger discovery was made during break at another campus café that served beer. According to that claim, the discovery of the bubble chamber idea was sparked by Donald Glaser at the University of Michigan while drinking a beer. Years later, I was upset during a visit to my grand daughter, who was a student at University of Michigan when I learned the place was replaced with a store, but I was more upset when I realized that the story, while being cute, is false. One consolation is that beer was used to fill bubble chambers to track elementary particles but was not the inspiration for the idea. Too bad for beer drinkers, and potential advertisers claiming that beer promotes discoveries.

Strickler and I shared the tiniest room I have ever seen, containing two small desks and two chairs. When one of us wanted to leave, the other person had to pull his chair inwards. The space, I can not call it room, had one advantage: a window which made it cheerful. It had one more constraint: to leave it one had to be careful when opening the wooden sliding door because it opens into the lab where experiments were carried out that required total darkness and that is why the walls, the curtains and the doors were painted black.

Besides Mecca there were other places for coffee breaks, including a small room adjoining the lab. This promoted close interaction within our research group.

Us four Egyptian chemistry graduate students often ate outside as none of us was fond of cooking. Since I was a new comer, I depended on the other two Egyptians who preceded us. One had a car which provided transportation. The only other alternative available only for short distances was walking. They knew where to go. One place we frequented was a restaurant that featured fried chicken long before Colonel Sanders and his mass produced Kentucky Fried Chickens. Favour's restaurant's specialty was fried chicken and it was delicious. The only problem was we needed lots of bread and the waitresses kept providing us with more bread. Egyptians consume lots of bread. In fact we call it "aish", literally meaning life. As the waitresses came to know us they automatically provided a huge quantity of bread.

Later, we discovered fancier restaurants, including the Silver Slipper. Their specialty was porter house steaks for only five dollars, an unimaginable price today! Another was Georges by the Gulf where we ate delicious flounder fish and hush puppies. Of course there were several Drive in restaurants. My preference was the one that had young beautiful women serving us on roller skates and wearing cow boy hats and hot pants! Nowadays one does not have to go to a drive in restaurant to watch girls with hot pants. They are all over the place, including universities. The difference is that nowadays the hot pants are torn blue denim tiny shorts.

One day I decided to treat my research group to a shish kabab feast. I learned the art from Moses, a Syrian grocer that I befriended. He taught me how to cut and marinate the meat, cut it into nice pieces and make "kufta" from minced lamb meat. The group immensely enjoyed the charcoal cooked meat. Needless to say, socialization whether over shish kabab or coffee breaks helped bringing down barriers and brought the research group closer and, more important, made us happier. A side effect, it promoted my English conversation.

One of the remarkable changes that happened in America the past few decades is the change in the variety of food that most Americans consume. In the Fifties, with the exception of cosmopolitan areas in large cities like New York, San Francisco, Chicago, Boston and New Orleans, most Americans had limited choices in food. Basically fried chicken, hamburger, steak, boiled rice, vegetables, corn, potatoes and, of course, apple pie. Exposure to the world through travel and arrival of immigrants from various countries, including those against which the USA waged war, helped in acquiring new tastes. Nowadays, wide varieties of international foods have become staples in supermarkets and are no longer limited to gourmet shops. Names like camembert, brie, gouda and manchego are among many other types of cheese that replaced the not particularly tasty American cheese. Likewise, fruits like mango, kiwi and dates became common. A few years ago, a wave of pizza and cappuccino gulping had swept the world. A wide variety of restaurants have opened and the number of Americans who eat outside have multiplied. Unfortunately, the consumption of fast food was accompanied with dramatic ill health effects; diabetes type II, obesity and various heart ailments. However, health awareness among the more educated has increased, together with the need for exercising. Thus gyms have become a fixture of modern America.

EPISODE EIGHTEEN:

At the Knickerbockers

I hesitated every time I said Knickerbockers to my Egyptian friends. It is not the "bocker" part of the word but the "knick" part that causes much hesitation. The word knick, which is pronounced without the k for reasons unknown to me, is very close to "neek", which in Arabic means "to make love" or more boldly, "to fuck". Before leaving Alexandria, I had a useful visit with my research professor who had his graduate and post-doctoral studies at American universities. He was, thus, quite familiar with aspects of American culture. He gave me advice on what to see in New York, including Radio City Music Hall, Forty Second and Broadway streets and recommended hotels to go to, one of which was the Knickerbockers Hotel at 45th street. So, before going to New York to meet my bride, I reserved at the Knickerbockers hotel for our first nights as newlyweds.

Before adolescence, I was told very briefly about the facts of life, that is about sexual intercourse. My first reaction was a mixture of shock and amusement. Soon enough, disgust and amusement were replaced by curiosity followed by excitement. I enjoyed love scenes that displayed some nudity both in American and Egyptian films. Seductive scenes of sexy movie stars like Egyptian actress Kamilia were sexier to me than the display of the prominent breasts of Jane Russell, but the seductiveness of Rita Heyworth or Salvana Mangano were something else.

I was happy to discover theological books in my father's modest library that dealt explicitly with the "etiquette of sexual intercourse in a religious framework". Of course, it was nothing like "The Perfumed Garden of Sheik Nafzawy" or the "Kama Sutra", which I read much later. Probably, I was one of a rare breed that got their introduction about sex from theological books. I had to be content with what was available and, more importantly, reading such books was not forbidden, but even encouraged. Thus, I read those specific chapters openly and I did not have to hide. Of course, my family did not know which chapters I was reading and were even surprised that I was interested in reading serious and not particularly amusing books. I was amazed as to the openness in dealing with various aspects of the subject from hygienic elements of the ritual of the intercourse, to how enjoyment of sex is alright and should not be accompanied with any feeling of guilt. Moreover, the book noted that sex is not merely for procreation, but also for pleasure.

Of course, the chapter was discussing sex strictly within marriage. It clearly emphasized that seeking joy in sex is not limited to the man, but is also the right of a woman. As a matter of fact, I learned that deprivation of a wife from sex for various reasons including impotence of the husband is a solid ground for divorce, which can be initiated by the woman. Masturbation is unfortunately forbidden. Moreover, various myths about the subject were popular. Prominent among them is that blindness is assured for those who frequently masturbated, and it was left vague what "frequently" exactly meant. I wondered how come blindness in my school and among my friends was rare! Recently, my nephew asked me about the threat of blindness resulting from masturbation. My response was to act as if I am blind. I closed my eyes and touched his face and said "Of course my son!"

Before arriving in the US I knew that the relationship between the sexes there is far more liberal than in Egypt. In fact, such liberty was exaggerated. My uncle, who was very liberal, warned me that I "should not expect to mount my date the first night". At FSU, the proportion of women to men was very high compared to other colleges not because the feminine mystique arrived prematurely but because FSU was previously a college for women. Actually, FSU was quite conservative, at least formally, given the realities of the Fifties. Dating followed certain rules: the male partner has to fetch his date on Friday or Saturday night from the exclusively women dorm or sorority, and she has to return by eleven, one hour before Cinderella time The scene surrounding female dorms few minutes before eleven was quite amusing. Tens of couples would kiss each other passionately and for long stretches. Obviously, it was assumed that the longer the kiss the better score one got. Breathing during such marathonic kisses was an art to master. However, the kisses were dry as Leon County which forbade liquor sales. Kisses also reflected the movies of the time, such as when the female date raises one leg during a kiss mimicking Ginger Rogers, which presumably added more delight. The scene resembles closely a flock of sea lions mating along the shore with one exception: activities do not have to cease at eleven. Well, there was another exception, real mating occurs between our mammalian cousins.

I could rationalize my venture into dating as a pre-marriage exercise, or admit that I wanted to go through the exercise out of curiosity or simply that I desired the company of a young beautiful woman. My colleague, Ali, apparently had similar thoughts as he was preparing to meet his fiancé who was scheduled to arrive in New York shortly. Having a car is decidedly a critical advantage for dating. He asked me to join him in a double date to the movies, which I accepted. That was when I met Mary Locker, a beautiful Canadian student. It was fun until I opened a delicate subject: segregation. "My big mouth", as Jackie Gleason would shout, condemned the practice in clear terms. The girls identified me as a Negro as she told Ali later. I had two dates with Mary that did not materialize into a relationship, physical or romantic. It was amusing to go to her dorm and wait in the lobby and get announced "Mary Locker you have a caller" so I could claim that I had a dating experience in America.

In preparation for marriage, I resorted to read a book on sexual facts. At that time, there were professional books written by doctors, nothing like today where a variety of books are available with photos of various positions, I have to contend with written descriptions and imagine the situation in my brain. Anyway, those books were very useful, especially discussions on the psychology of sex related to women and men.

Another step was to move from my current apartment that I shared with my companion from Egypt and find a separate apartment. I found a reasonably priced apartment very close to the chemistry building and on a street with many pecan trees. I enjoyed being alone and free to eat, clean and sleep when I wanted to especially since my previous room mate was not fun to be with. I also worked very hard to finish my research required for my Masters.

Everything was set to go and I took a train to New York. Soo Soo was scheduled to arrive at Idlewild Airport which is now called John F. Kennedy (JFK) Airport. I was very excited. Soo Soo finally emerged from customs as beautiful as ever. We hugged, collected her bags and off we went to the Knickerbockers. Talking about several items took most of our time interrupted by kisses and hugs.

Our activities were dominated by seeing standard tourist attractions in New York. So we had a dizzying ride on the fast elevator leading to the top of the Empire State Building viewing New York from above, walked along Broadway and Forty Second streets, saw Grand Central Station and the relatively new UN building which was completed in 1950. Soo Soo was thrilled, and particularly when we visited the Metropolitan Museum of Arts and specially the magnificent Ancient Egyptian collection. Particular joy was clear when she saw the spectacular Rockettes at Radio City Music Hall. We took a boat ride to see the skyline of New York and visit the Statue of Liberty. Most people know that the statue was a gift of from the people of France to the United States, but few realize that the statue was originally intended to be at the entrance of the Suez Canal in Egypt. The French sculptor Frédéric Bartholdi was so impressed with Egypt and ancient Egyptian monuments. However, Egypt was broke after the price of cotton collapsed after the American Civil War and Southern cotton poured into the international market. Revenues from the Suez Canal were not helpful since most of the revenue went to European investors. Only then was Bartholdi's statue radically changed from Lady Egypt to the current western looking Lady Liberty and American donors footed the bill.

My friend Mostafa was in town, and the three of us went to Coney Island, which is technically no longer an island, but who cares. Our objective was to have fun and fun we got. The amusement park was the background, but the laughter and the joy was generated by us. Of course, we laughed at trivial things. My bride had been in the States a couple of days and obviously she was fascinated with everything, which reminded me of my first few days in New York.

We ate hot dogs and laughed at the name but we enjoyed the taste. We ate ice cream and compared the taste with the delicious ice cream we regularly ate in Alexandria.

So it was a touristic trip more than a honeymoon. We had preliminary sexual activities but genuine enjoyable sex free of worries came later when we reached our home in Tallahassee. The few days we spent together in New York brought us together and initiated a happy bond that grew over the years.

Short of money, we decided to take the bus rather than the more expensive train. Soo Soo's flexibility was a good sign of not being fussy or aloof. When the bus crossed into the South, the so called "Dixie Line", Black Americans had to move to the back, which left us with an awful feeling and puzzlement, even though our conscientiousness as far as race issues was not fully developed at that time, particularly Soo Soo's who had just arrived.

Finally, we arrived to our apartment. Our honeymoon began even though in a few days Soo Soo would start her freshman year and I would have to finish my masters and move to Michael Kasha's lab. We had mostly good memories of those days. Needless to say, lots of adjustments were needed and some quarrels happened that sometimes brought tears to Soo Soo and made her walk out collecting pecans falling from the trees along our street. Quarrels in any close relationship serve a crucial function, excreting tension and anger leading to more solid relations with a critical condition that the quarrel does not become a match of hitting below the belt or hurtful insults.

EPISODE NINETEEN:

Quiz Show

There we were in New York again. We were free from worries. Soheir was on her way to finishing her Bachelor's degree in bacteriology the next summer and I was progressing along in my research and course work. We were both happy and willing to try new things, so we decided to get tickets to watch a quiz show at NBC Studios. The notion that we would be picked to compete was a remote possibility, but it was not totally absent from our minds. We sat in the middle of the room with other spectators, and were coached by a person telling us when to applaud and when to stop. He started to select contestants and, to our total surprise, as well as delight, and with clear eyes of envy from the rest of the viewers, we were chosen. We were asked to change our seats and move to specially assigned ones that actually did not provide us with a good view of the set, but who cared? I whispered to my wife that even if we lost, as was most likely expected, we would get a few valuable appliances. Neither I nor my wife cared to know the answers to the type of questions that test knowledge of trivial or unimportant facts. The man from the show came to me and asked for our shipping address to send the items that we would win and added that we might regret getting them in view of the taxes we would have to pay. We did not have any money to spare for such taxes but I planned to get a loan. We were in a materialistic mood, amplified by the raised expectations to win some valuable items. The show went on and the audience followed the instructions religiously, applauding when the sign was given to do so. We felt awkward joining the crowd and we skipped some of the applause. We desperately waited to be called, but that did not happen. The show was over and we expected that we would be asked to come back on another day, which would force us to change our travel plans. Nobody came so I went to the person in charge to inquire about our participation in the future. He said it was over. Period. The quick switch from a friendly smiling mode to an irritated, cold mode was distinct. We were left with mixed feelings: on one hand, disappointment for leaving empty handed; and on the other, we realized that we were used by the managers of the show. The selection process was fake, designed to give an illusion that it was genuine.

Years later, I saw the film "Quiz Show", which was based on Goodwin's "Remembering America" and featured Ralph Fiennes and John Turturro. During the film, flashbacks from our 1959 personal episode at NBC Studios in New York kept coming. The film was based on a real story, that of Van Doren who was a professor at Colombia University and who was a contestant on a quiz show called "Twenty One". He was reluctant to participate at first, but ended up to be a regular on the show as he kept winning. He was deliberately chosen by the producers of the show to lift the declining ratings. The idea was that his image as an intellectual image and his respected family background would be a boost to the show. This was crucial for the simple reason that the ratings were falling and, thus, advertisement money was shrinking. This was blamed on another contestant, Herb Stempel, who lacked the personality and appeal but kept winning. "Stempel must be replaced at all costs", thought the producers, who were obviously guided by the pursuit of money and "success" without regard to ethics or principles. They decided to rig the show by asking Stempel to deliberately give wrong answers so that he would be replaced by Van Doren not unlike asking a boxer to deliberately fall and lose a fight and miss the chance to be a "contender" as Marlon Brando expressed it in a memorable line in the movie "On the Waterfront". In return, Stempel, played magnificently by John Turturro, was promised a spot on a TV panel show. Van Doren became a star thanks to the media that displayed his photos in Life and Time magazines. Sure enough, the ratings improved and everyone was happy. However, Stempel was furious when the producers reneged on their promise to him and the entire plot fell apart and backfired.

The rigging was exposed and a full blown scandal emerged, which led to a Congressional investigation. All quiz shows were then subjected to scrutiny for a while. One interesting aspect that was displayed in the story was the self deceit that intellectuals sometimes engage in armed with an ample reservoir of rationales and justifications. Van Doren had to resign his university post, but at NBC the directors used a standard line: "We had no prior knowledge". One must assert that corruption does not exist solely in the media, but also in politics, sports and even in science and it is also not local, but global.

EPISODE TWENTY:

From Cruising the Nile to Viewing Niagara Falls

"Traveling has seven benefits." So states the Arabic proverb. In reality though it has a multitude of joys and pleasures and I would not be exaggerating if I say that travel is a major component of life because it changes and widens the scope of one's life. This conviction was elevated to a major priority not only in my own life, but also in the lives of my children and grandchildren. Travel to some may mean the motion of flying to different places, lodging in fancy hotels and visiting standard sites, including tourist traps. To me it is all that and much more. It is mixing with people of different cultures, eating native food, and hearing various accents and languages, learning about different customs and myths and enjoying various types of music, dances and songs without necessarily understanding the lyrics.

Before coming to the States, my travels were always with my family. I do not forget the excitement of being told that we will go to Cairo or Alexandria or even short trips around the various cities that we lived in every four years when my father was transferred to a different city as the top civil engineer in the Survey Department. That exposed me to different places in Egypt, and gave me the opportunity to visit different environments and see several ancient Egyptian monuments, as well as different mosques and churches with different histories and architectures.

When my father was demoted and exiled to the South for political reasons, we stayed behind in Tanta in the middle of the Delta to complete our school year. Soon after, we joined my father in Luxor during the long summer vacation. Luxor is very hot in the summer, but dry, which makes the heat more tolerable as long as one is in the shade.

Before sunset, my brother and I would go down and sit by the river Nile. Usually there was one or two men throwing their nets in the water to catch fish, mostly Bolti (Talapia) a native tasty fish eaten either fried or blackened over direct fire after being covered with coarse wheat powder. It is then eaten after squeezing lemon on it and some people like to put red hot pepper (shattah). Sometimes it is cooked in the oven after mixing with various spices as well as tomato sauce, only then it deserves to be called "kosbareyah". We enjoyed watching the fishermen by the river. Often we were asked to try our luck by giving the fisherman one piaster and in return we were entitled to take all the fish he caught after one throw of the net or leave empty handed if he got nothing. Most of the time it was the latter. This was like a lottery called "yanaseeb", meaning your luck, but the odds were better than Power Ball. One can imagine our excitement when a fish was caught and seeing it struggling and wiggling to escape.

Another spectacle that my brother and I looked forward to seeing every other day was the landing of a passenger plane over the Nile. The amphibious aircraft first appeared in the sky, and eventually it aligned with the Nile, its runway. The landing occurred with a big water splash that caused a wave that traveled to both banks of the Nile forcing all the boats to move in resonance with the water wave. That event gave us a thrill every time we watched. After landing, motor boats approached the plane and whisked rich tourists to the bank of the river facing the Winter Palace Hotel. Luggage followed later and formalities related to passports and visas were taken care of while guests sipped cold hibiscus drink (karkadee). Not only is it a delicious drink, but it lowers blood pressure. Winter Palace is indeed a palace with its magnificent interior, luxurious rooms overlooking the Nile or beautiful gardens with different types of palm trees and a large swimming pool. King Farouk had a special suite overlooking the Nile. This was recently occupied by Sarkozy, the former President of France. The hotel garden was the site where he made out with his girlfriend. This caused many brows to be raised in disgust and disapproval from the hotel attendants who witnessed his performance.

As children in Luxor, we were not bored at all. As soon as the sun set and the weather became pleasant, we had plenty to do: walking by the corniche of the Nile, taking a horse carriage that raced along the Nile, or visiting the nearby formidable Luxor temple. Little did we know then that under our feet as we walked into one of the halls of the Temple was a treasure hidden underground that was later discovered, and included magnificent statues of pharaohs, some of them perfectly preserved. The "khabeeah" as it was called, which literally means "hidden", is exhibited and nicely displayed in a special museum in Luxor along the Nile.

The climax of our stay in Luxor that summer was undoubtedly our family boat trip. My father used the opportunity to show us most of the Egyptian monuments in the South. We took a trip in a motor boat along the Nile and slept cramped in the boat, but who cared, particularly for us children. We stopped at various cities, visited monuments, and ate local food, including fresh fish from the Nile cooked in different styles, dates and yogurt served in locally made pots, which gave it a unique taste. We also ate famous local molasses, which we call black honey, sometimes mixed with sesame paste called "taheena". Black honey is not only delicious but very healthy. Our parents encouraged us to eat it as it is particularly rich in potassium, iron, magnesium and calcium.

We enjoyed magic nights gazing at millions of stars in the clear sky and wondering about the universe, and enjoying the cool breeze at night in compensation for the sizzling heat in the day time. Traveling along the Nile has a magic aspect given the many myths surrounding the magnificent river. As we traveled, we saw male peasants using ancient tools ("shadoof") to transfer water from the Nile to their plots. Some were completely nude, which brought giggles and was a source of amusement and perhaps excitement to the young women servants who accompanied us. We enjoyed passing through locks as we reached several dams across the Nile. The water level was lower as we crossed the dam to the North and we had to wait until the water level dropped to the level in front of the dam. That trip was the first introduction to our ancient history, assisted by a nice detailed guide to the temples and tombs that we visited. We visited old ancient Egyptian temples as well as temples built during the Ptolemy (Greek) rule. It was noticeable how the engravings on the walls did not approximate the artistry and refinement of earlier temples. What a trip it was, combining fun, knowledge, as well as cultural exposure.

My youngest brother was newly born and had the habit of farting with a loud noise, which was very embarrassing to those near him and made them take a few steps away lest they were blamed for the noise. One time we were visiting the sanctuary of the temple that leads to progressively larger halls for decreasing status and larger crowds. So sounds at the sacred sanctuary would amplify as a result of the horn like effect. My infant brother chose to use the moment to produce one of his loud farts. This time he had the benefit of amplification via the temple horn effect.

As kids, we were startled to see on the walls of several temples the God of Fertility with an erected penis in faded red color. Noticeable also were topless dancers and singers in vivid colors that did not fade as these were in underground tombs protected from sunlight. Not only did ancient Egyptian culture permit such nudity, we were also presented with pornographic drawings and images as I discovered many years later. The most famous is the erotic papyrus in the Turin museum of Italy that was exhibited lately in the Louvre in Paris. Various partly comical sex scenes in vivid colors are shown in the papyrus. Ancient Egyptians had fun as well as a sense of humor that manifests itself till today as modern Egyptians are known for their jokes about all aspect of life, including sex, politics, marriage as well as the ironies of life.

I learned quite recently of the "Festival of Drunkenness" where Egyptians had a day of drinking beer and having sex to commemorate a myth when angry Gods sent the goddess "Hathor" in the form of a lioness "Sekhmet" to punish them. She drank their blood and became unstoppable so God made beer with the color of blood which made her drunk and people were saved.

At night when most were asleep and it was perfectly quiet, we enjoyed the full moon as its reflection on the Nile added an exotic beauty, specially when the water subtly moved as if it was in a romantic dance with the distant moon. When boats carrying pottery and molasses approached, the tempo of the dance was enhanced. Relaxing and gazing at the water and the quivering moon reflections was like a massage of the soul.

As we traveled south towards Aswan, the Nile became narrower and wilder. The captain (Rayyes) had to navigate through huge granite rocks, some of which having ancient inscriptions. The ride was thrilling and showed how el-rayyes was skilled and knew every turn of the river. However it appears wild, the modern Nile is very tame compared to the Ancient Nile, and by ancient I mean very ancient, as in millions of years ago. It remained wild until recently, perhaps ten thousand years ago, when it became tame enough for people to move to the valley.

There were other long trips that followed my boat trip to the US. Upon arriving in Tallahassee, we immediately became busy taking entrance examinations and started the Fall semester with several courses. We did not think about traveling except during our first Christmas break. An Egyptian colleague, Ali, also a graduate student in Chemistry and Mostafa who preceded us at Florida State University by more than a year, decided to go to New Orleans. Ali had a huge Buick, the broadest model ever made. My colleague Abdo and I joined them and drove to the charming city. Ali drove fast, and we were stopped by the police once. We got into a heavy mist that was DDT spray that made visibility very poor. In fact, Jane Mansfield, the actress famous for her exposed large breasts, was killed in a car accident under similar circumstances a few years later. She was heading to New Orleans when her Buick car hit the rear of a truck and went under it. The truck was moving slowly due to heavy spraying of mosquito pesticide that dimmed visibility. Since then, trucks are required to put a steel bar to prevent passenger cars from going under in cases of rear collisions. The bar is ironically called the Mansfield bar.

Surprisingly, we arrived safely in New Orleans. The main attraction was the French Quarter and burlesque shows, walking down Bourbon Street, passing by numerous nightclubs where men stood outside to encourage passersby to enter so they would open a screen that allowed you to see semi nude women dancing and say "just started, just started". We were amused and "just started" became our mantra during and after the trip. We eventually entered one night club and immediately women came to our table and ordered drinks and started teasing us sexually. Frankly, I was turned off. We did not go to fancy restaurants as we were graduate students on limited budgets, but we had a taste of Creole cooking, which is a mixture of European and African cuisines.

We saw a funeral with a musical band which immediately reminded me of the amazing similarity with the Hassaballah band in Egypt that marched in front of funerals. In New Orleans you can not escape hearing jazz music and listening to Louis Armstrong. I liked jazz from the beginning, but did not enjoy Creole cuisine. Perhaps I was not properly introduced to its dishes.

A year or so after my New Orleans trip I got married. While both of us became busy in our studies, a window of time had opened to embark on a short trip as a couple. One of my American colleagues who had been camping in the Smoky Mountains urged us to camp there. He even lent us a tent and suggested a spot which he said was not usually crowded. So we took our newly acquired 1949 black Dodge, and got necessary maps. No GPS was available then. We became overwhelmed with how beautiful the scenery was as we approached the Smokies. We quickly realized how the name accurately matched the breathless scenery with fog at the top of the mountains. We had difficulty erecting the tent, but we finally managed. On the first night in the tent we got a big scare. A huge black bear searching for food paid us a visit. We ran to our car and locked it. Cars at that time were made of thick steel not like modern cars that can be easily crushed, so we felt safe. In the morning, we explored the park and picked an interesting spot to have lunch. We had to go down hill to reach a stream hidden by the thick surrounding forest and we sat in the cool water. We imagined Native Americans who hunted here, before Europeans came and colonized the area, enjoying swimming nude in the stream and perhaps making love.

Our Italian colleague and his wife were also camping nearby. We met them by coincidence and mentioned our episode with the bear who came to our tent for dinner. Not long after our adventure, the "Smokies" became a number one hit song with lyrics like: "Don't let Smokey mountain smoke get in your eyes .. If you do I'm telling you .. You'll want to live there the rest of your life.. If Smokey Mountain smoke gets in your eyes". That was a most enjoyable trip, particularly that it was the first trip with my wife.

Another longer trip with my wife took us up north along the East Coast. We stopped at several beaches that did not impress us at all compared to the beautiful beaches of Alexandria and Marsa Matrouh on the northwest coast of Egypt. The latter was the favorite swimming place of Cleopatra and there are beaches named after her there. Eventually we reached Washington DC where we visited friends and few monuments, and then we headed for New York. We stayed again at Knickerbockers Hotel, met our Egyptian friends, went to a quiz TV show and of course walked along Broadway. Our visit to New York had a different flavor as we became more experienced and more familiar with the American society.

As we traveled further up north my dream to view Niagara Falls became a reality. It was very romantic as we recalled the movie with Marilyn Monroe. I became fixated on the desire to visit the falls since I saw the film in Alexandria. I recalled the scene of Marilyn Monroe humming and singing with her sexy red dress and her lips driving men crazy. It is amazing how that scene was seductive without nudity or explicit sex. To me that is art. I also recalled some of the lyrics of that historic scene:

> *Kiss, kiss me, Hold, hold me…*
> *Say you miss, miss me*
> *Kiss me love, with heavenly affection*
> *Hold, hold me close to you Hold me, see me through*
> *With all your heart's protection*
> *Thrill, thrill me with your charms*
> *Take me, in your arms and make my life perfection*
> *Kiss, kiss me darling Then, kiss me once again…*

We were told many stories such as those who attempted to go over the falls using specially designed barrels. Few of them succeeded and many perished. Some died in accidents, including Joseph Cotton in the movie. A number of stunts were attempted including walking on a rope across the falls. Tourist guides repeated facts about the Falls, which we forgot before the tour was completed. We were mesmerized by the tremendous volume of the water that goes over the Falls and its height. When we returned the shoes and the yellow coats at the end of the tour, scenes from the movie flashed in our minds as Monroe's lover was killed on a nearby spot by the jealous husband.

We proceeded to reach Columbus, Ohio in time where I joined our research group to attend the Annual Spectroscopy Conference. The sudden change from Niagara to Columbus represented an anticlimax, particularly to my wife who was alone during the conference proceeding. I, on the other hand, looked with great anticipation and excitement to those proceedings. Listening to the latest advances in the field from the leading scientists and meeting them personally was thrilling to me as a young scientist.

As the conference drew to its conclusion, we started our trip back to Tallahassee driving my 1949 Dodge. Three of my colleagues joined me and my wife. It was delightful to head back home to the usual routine, but armed with few new ideas that I was eager to test experimentally. We were laughing and gossiping when suddenly the temperature gauge of the car went wild. Obviously, something serious happened at a very bad time. We were at the top of the mountains at night and it was raining heavily. Luckily, we were close to a motel. One of us volunteered to walk in the rain to fetch a car mechanic. Later, he got a severe cold in reward of his valiant act. We gathered the cash that all of us had. It was barely enough to cover the rental of only one room as we had to keep enough to cover the cost of repair and gas for the remainder of the trip. The following morning it was sunny and bright. The car had a new head on gasket and we recovered our cheerful mood as we continued our drive to Tallahassee. Being the driver and the owner of the car I was relieved when we finally arrived.

EPISODE TWENTY-ONE:

Sheneda

My wife graduated with a B.Sc. degree in Bacteriology from Florida State University, and she was in her seventh month of pregnancy with our first child that we both hoped to be a girl. In those days, one could not predict the sex of the fetus as ultrasound scans were not invented yet. In various cultures, however, there are numerous ways of guessing. These include prediction based on the shape of the abdomen and a few other methods. The Ancient Egyptians used an interesting technique based on the germination of a specific seed after it was drenched with the pregnant woman's urine. None of those techniques were reliable in spite of assertions to the contrary by ardent believers. The fact that such predictions were correct half of the time meant nothing since there were only two possibilities. Nevertheless, it was an amusing exercise to make predictions, provided that they were not taken too seriously. Nowadays, most parents get their surprise as to the sex of their new child moved up by a few months. Interestingly, millions initially doubted the ability of ultrasonic scans to identify the sex of a fetus on the grounds that this is solely in the realm of God's knowledge. Now such a notion has essentially evaporated.

We were granted our wish in early August 1959, and were blessed with a lovely girl whom we named Gigi. Yes, we were influenced by the delightful film "Gigi", which was shown around that time. Gigi is the nickname, but the real name is Jehan, Persian for World. Shah Jahan, which means King of the World was indeed the fifth and greatest ruler of the Mughal Empire of the early Seventeenth Century. He is famous for the Taj Mahal at Agra in India, which is the tomb of his wife Mumtaz, symbolizing his love and affection for her, as well as the Peacock Throne. When I visited the Taj Mahal many years later, I felt a sensation of love and spirituality, a sort of transcendental experience. The beautiful white, translucent marble was alive and reflected the strong affection Shah Jahan had for his wife. There was a strong feeling of sadness as well, since he was deposed and imprisoned in a fort by his son. Shah Jahan would view the tomb of his beloved wife from his nearby prison until his death when he finally joined his wife in the Taj Mahal.

The birth of Gigi transformed our life and brought great happiness to us, and, with Soheir's graduation, we were looking forward to a period of financial sufficiency and even some savings. During the previous three years, we were drained by tuition fees, including the larger out of state tuition. I remember the struggle every semester to get the large sum of out of state tuition waived, but only with occasional success. The administrator who had the power to grant such a waiver was an unfriendly lady who consistently refused our request. We had to borrow from the Lewis State Bank. Luckily, the Lewis Brothers, who were friendly to foreign students in general, were quite helpful and trusting, especially since we always paid our loans on time. When we gathered our courage and went directly to the Dean, we got some or all of the tuition waived. We wished that we had discovered that understanding Dean earlier. We were strained financially even though we had an allowance paid by the Egyptian Government that made our monthly income one hundred dollars more than other graduate students. At that time, a research assistantship paid around $150 per month. To put the situation in perspective, I must mention that three pounds of ground beef cost one dollar, a movie theatre ticket was only a quarter, a domestic mail stamp was three cents and our very expensive one bedroom air conditioned apartment was $60 per month. We anticipated an additional income from Soheir's job as a technical assistant with a famous botanist from Germany, who was studying photosynthesis. Now our income nearly tripled and we could pay off our loans. We even began to buy items that we always wanted to acquire, such as a fancy stereo speaker system with an elaborate turntable. Moreover, with the birth of Gigi we became eligible to move to university housing at Mayberry

Heights. These were basically wooden cottages, which were convenient, nicely located and very cheap, thirty five dollars a month. All our neighbors were graduate students, some of them foreign families, but mostly American families and two other Egyptian families lived in the neighborhood.

During the summer, Soheir was not working yet. Thus, Gigi was taken care of full time by an elated mother who was in ecstasy to have a baby girl, giving her baths, feeding her, playing with her and singing to her. I too enjoyed taking photos of her, putting her to sleep and spending most of my spare time with her. After a few months, we gave her early swimming lessons in the bathtub which gave her a head start in swimming, which she enjoyed immensely. Later, however, when a "smart" adult told her that there were biting fish in the water she developed an inhibition to getting into the water. It took several months to get rid of such inhibition.

That time was an important phase in my graduate work, preparing for comprehensive examinations and working hard on my research, which required very long hours of experimental work, sometimes requiring late hours in the lab. All around, things looked very bright indeed. It was easy to forget the unspoken but alarming reality. We were living in a split society, one part for "Colored", another for "Whites". We rarely saw "Colored" people or came in touch with them, except when we went to the Win-Dixie food store. There was not a single black American family living in the neighborhoods that we lived in. FSU was lily-white without a single black faculty member or a single student, undergraduate or graduate. The football team's players, the "Seminoles", were all white. Other than the few blacks on campus who were janitors or garbage collectors, we lived in a monochromatic society. How easy it was to get used to an anomaly disguised as reality. Occasionally though, I was quietly reminded with reality when an old black janitor in the department would step aside to let me pass him. When I insisted that he walk ahead of me because it was his right, and out of respect for his age, the man had a puzzled look on his face, probably surprised by the ignorance of a young foreign student.

When Soheir started work, we needed someone to take care of Gigi. A neighbor highly recommended her baby sitter that she no longer needed anymore as they were leaving town. Sheneda started baby sitting for Gigi and we were pleased primarily for the genuine love she expressed for her and later for the positive reaction of Gigi when she came in the morning. Sheneda loved her and gave her genuine care and affection. I forgot to mention that Sheneda was African-American, or a "Negro" using the standard word of the time. She was fat and had a cheerful face that reminded me with Aunt Jemima of pancake fame and the black actress in "Gone with the Wind", who played the part of a nanny who took care of Scarlet. Soheir and I liked Sheneda and were happy that she was taking care of Gigi. She stayed with us for a long time, and became a friend.

I naturally gave Sheneda a ride home, which gave me an opportunity to discuss with her a number of issues. Her residence in a black (Negro) neighborhood of Tallahassee allowed me to have some idea of that section of town. Tallahassee's growth lead to concentric bands of black and white. There was a band where Negroes lived, surrounded with a band where whites had nice homes. As the city grew, new concentric bands developed, just like Newton's rings in physics, a phenomenon resulting from diffraction of light waves. When waves overlap in phase, a light ring forms. When waves are out of phase, a black ring forms. The analogy is indeed appropriate.

One day, some American neighbors, who were white of course, gave me some stern advice: "The custom here is to have Negroes sit in the back of the car if you have to give them a ride". I refused the advice angrily. That upset my neighbors, but, after a while, they grudgingly accepted my stand. Reflecting on the incident later I was amused since people of high status everywhere usually sit in the back, diagonal to the driver. Rich and famous people and those who hold important business or government positions, including those who pretend to be important, always sit in that privileged position. In fact, my father, who had an important government position as a civil engineer, always sat in that position when he was driven to and from his work. So, in a funny way, Sheneda had been inadvertently demoted by sitting beside me in the car. It is amazing how President Eisenhower and Sheneda would have the same car position when driven to their respective homes. Of course, the implication in both situations is orthogonal. The custom was consistent with the desire of whites to keep a clear distance from "Negros" except in intimate, usually forced, encounters.

When Sheneda began to trust me, she openly expressed her feelings of anger and abhorrence of segregation and injustice. When I told her of my naivety regarding blacks in America when I first came to the US and how I assumed that blacks had equal rights since Lincoln, she laughed. A special laughter was reserved for my story about the Colored water fountain that I encountered on my first day in Tallahassee. She had admiration for Nasser as an African leader who had a keen sense of social justice. She explained how Jim Crow laws enacted in 1876 formalized segregation in the Southern and border states. These infamous laws severely restricted the civil rights of Black Americans who were degraded to second-class citizens in the "Land of the Free".

She also told me several stories of rapes of black women by white men. One of the postdoctoral students in our group told us one day how his white neighbor returned home early while his working wife was absent and chased the screaming black maid during an apparent sexual assault. It seems such incidents were not rare and history confirms this. For some the slogan "Separate But Equal", translated into "Intimate But Unequal", which better described the situation. Sheneda told me a most astonishing story from oral black history which was denied by many whites. One of the Founding Fathers of the US, Thomas Jefferson, had a black mistress teenager named Sally Hemings. Even though the relationship was exposed and used politically against Jefferson, history somehow laundered the affair. Recent DNA analysis settled the controversy and confirmed Jefferson's paternity of Sally's children. Sally herself was the daughter of Jefferson's father in- law, her mother was his slave mistress and Jefferson's wife inheritance. Ironically, Jefferson was an advocate of keeping white blood pure and, thus, was against race-mixing consistent with White Supremacy ideals, although Jefferson fulfilled his promise to his mistress by freeing her children.

Sheneda introduced me to a newspaper entitled "Mohammed Speaks" which is the voice of The Nation of Islam. Sheneda read the paper regularly even though she was not a Black Muslim. Naturally, I was curious to learn more about The Nation of Islam, their history, beliefs, philosophy, their stands on various issues and particularly the degree of overlap with traditional Islam. One of their teachings is that W.D. Farad Muhammad is the "Messiah of Christianity and the Mahdi of Islam". Farad is believed to have disappeared mysteriously after he transmitted his revelation to the new messenger, Elijah Mohammed, who led the "Nation" until he died in 1975. It was clear to me that he advocated beliefs that are contrary to traditional Islam. The deification of any human being contradicts a basic tenant of Islam that emphasizes that Prophet Mohammad is but a human being and had no Godly attributes. That is the reason why Moslems adamantly refuse being referred to as Mohammedans. Traditional Islam considers Mohammed, the Messenger of God, as the last one in a line of prophets and messengers that include Moses and Jesus. For Moslems, the Torah and the Bible are sacred books and are revelations from the same God ("Allah" in Arabic). Also, Islam never advocates the preference of one race over another. When Moslems pray, all stand in one line without any distinction of class or race. Such an exercise of equality is significant even though it is symbolic. As soon as the prayers are over the crowd scatters and falls back to their respective social or, more accurately, class niches, although a residual practice of equality of varying degrees persists. So considering whites as "blue-eyed devils" is completely alien to the fundamentals of Islam.

Under the banner of "Separate but Equal" in the apartheid South all facilities and institutions were segregated. That included schools, universities, churches, sports activities, clubs, restaurants, hotels and motels. It was obvious to me that the teachings of the Nation of Islam, including separatist ideology, emerged as a reaction to the untold cruelty and injustice that befell blacks. Political, business, educational and media institutions were dominated by whites, so essentially all power not only in the South but also the North was in their hands. Effectively, the slogan that better describes the situation was "Separate and Unequal". Sheneda explained how black men were emasculated, when an old black man was called by a young or old white man "Hey Boy" he was expected to quickly answer "Yes Sir" or "Yes Boss". Such injustices were even rationalized by religion with the claim that if God wanted us equal He would have created all people in the same color. Thus, it was not surprising to see separate black and white churches of the same denomination, although the Catholic Church in Tallahassee allowed blacks in the balcony. I always rejected any ideology or religion that advocates separatism or advocates monochromatic societies, racial superiority, exceptionalism and manifest destinies. The notion that whites were the result of techniques developed by Yakub, a black scientist, to rule for thousands of years through lies, tricks, deceit and "divide and conquer" manipulations is extremely troubling to say the least. It mixes myth with partial realities and in a way it hinders the confrontation of exploitation, slavery and oppression. Baffling stories of the Ezekiel's Mother Wheel for UFO built on the island of Nippon (Japan) at a cost of billions of dollars in gold being used to raise mountains on Earth must amuse geologists particularly. Obviously, black Islam adopted myths as a counter to white myths and untold crimes and injustices committed by many whites. Nevertheless, the Nation of Islam undoubtedly promoted black pride and brought dignity, discipline and motivation to thousands of blacks attracted to the Nation. After the death of Elijah Mohammad, the Nation of Islam split, with a faction led by Louis Farrakhan. The other faction was led by Elijah's son W.D. Mohammad who disbanded the militaristic security force called "The Fruit of Islam". He steered his group away from the idea of a separate black nation towards traditional main stream Islam. He also shed off a number of key beliefs and courageously announced that Farad was not God, and that Elijah Mohammad, his father, was not a prophet. He said that his common sense told him that such claims were ridiculous. Farrakhan was implicated in the assassination of the radical leader Malcolm X when Malcolm ran into disfavor with Elijah Mohammad. Later in his life, Malcolm had converted to traditional Islam and went to Mecca for pilgrimage and visited Egypt. I heard Malcolm X speak in Boston before his conversion to traditional Islam, and had a brief discussion with him on the subject. I also heard Louis Farrakhan in Washington many years later. I was not impressed by the way his young followers all dressed the same with a bow tie. The Muslim Brotherhood similarly controlled their public gatherings with control disguised as discipline. Such behavior recalls fascist organizations in the last century that demanded blind obedience. This stunts free, critical thinking and inhibits the pursuit of knowledge and, most dangerously, transforms most young adherents into convenient robots. My conclusions are not theoretical ones, but are derived from long practical experience with students in Alexandria University where many students belonged to the Muslim Brotherhood since the late Seventies. More dangerously, the Muslim Brotherhood also had a secret military branch that carried out violent acts and assassination in the Forties.

I must emphasize, however, that the plight and grievances of blacks in America was and is real. Disagreeing with approaches such as that of The Nation of Islam should not be a cover to rationalize or escape from dark and ugly realities.

Sheneda was not only a loving nanny, she also taught me a number of things, but, above all, she gave me an opportunity to know a delightful bright black American woman. Until today, we have good memories of Sheneda and we often mention her to Gigi who was the prime recipient of her love, affection and kindness.

EPISODE TWENTY-TWO:

Excitement of Science: From Tadpoles to Luminescence

My arrival in the USA signified an exciting beginning in many ways, like a silk worm undergoing an abrupt metamorphosis into a colorful butterfly. Suddenly, I shed the confinement of my comfortable warm and secure cocoon and entered a much wider space that gave me the potential of viewing and sampling various flowers, sweet as well as sour. Not only was I eager to explore many things with an open mind, but also to make my own choices and discard others. My excitement for life had a central component, which was the excitement of science.

Upon my arrival at Florida Stat University, I had to take a battery of tests: a placement test in all four branches of chemistry in order to identify the courses required to bolster my background; and graduate record examinations in general science, mathematics, history, music and cultural knowledge, which included questions about Beethoven, Mozart, Kant and other Western philosophers. Not surprisingly, I did badly on this examination. I was angry to the point that I requested an appointment with the Chairman of the Chemistry Department, Dr. Karl Dittmer.

I had already heard positive things about him from the two Egyptian graduate students in the department who came one year ahead of us. As a matter of fact, he was responsible for recruiting the first Egyptian graduate student in the department five years earlier. As a consultant to a beer company, he met Ezzat Younathan who was on a short mission from Egypt to update Government quality control measures. Apparently Dr. Dittmer was impressed by him and saw him as a good candidate for a PhD in Biochemistry, in spite of the fact that he received his BSc several years before. Well, he was right. Ezzat proved to be an excellent student and successfully finished his graduate work with Dr. Earl Frieden. His success prompted two professors to offer fellowships to two other Egyptians, one of whom became a prominent physical chemistry professor and Editor of the prestigious Journal of Physical Chemistry. Their success in turn led to the offering of two additional fellowships, one of which was awarded to me.

Dr. Dittmer had a strong amiable personality. As a good leader he listened attentively to my blunt argument about the cultural specificity of the GRE to which he showed both respect and some amusement. I asked him if he knew about a prominent collection of scientists, philosophers, poets, musicians and singers from my cultural background, such as Almutanabi, Abu Alaa Almaari, Sayed Darwish, Abdelwahab, Um Kalthoum, Ibn Aalhayan, Alnafisi or Ikhwan Alsafaa. He said none or very little. I responded, you have just failed that part of the examination. I was pleasantly surprised when he told me that he got the point and would recommend that the culturally specific parts of the examination be canceled for foreign students. One can not help but admire people like Dr. Dittmer, for he reflected real leadership and a high degree of self confidence that allowed him to make bold decisions and reevaluate established requirements. How much I wish that contemporary leaders would have such qualities!

My first meeting with my biochemistry professor was not encouraging. He seemed socially awkward and uninspiring. From the beginning, I got the impression that he was eager to make clear that productive research work leading to publications was his main expectation. To make matters worse he assigned me to a project dealing with tadpoles. I was supposed to attend to these relatively huge tadpoles, change the water in which they swam and provide them with food containing specific doses of thyroxin. Thyroxin, a hormone secreted by thyroid glands, accelerates the normal process of their metamorphosis into frogs. Such a dramatic change from being an aquatic organism to one that lives mainly on land, must involve dramatic biochemical changes not least of which is the change of the respiratory system from using gills to lungs. Other drastic changes involve a complete shrinkage of the tail and full development of four limbs. Logically, this provided a good model to study some of the chemical changes associated with development in general. One troubling fact was that this area of research did not interest me as I was far more interested in physical chemistry. Nevertheless, I accepted the Biochemistry fellowship hoping that I would work on a topic closer to my interests. Eventually, the death rate of tadpoles under my care climbed significantly, so my professor switched me to another project more to my liking. I was not a tadpole serial killer, but my unconscious neglect to change the water probably led to such deaths.

Across the corridor from the laboratory, there was a charismatic professor who worked on an exciting topic that fit exactly into my interests. Dr. Michael Kasha had an interesting group investigating luminescence of materials when they were excited by a beam of light. These experiments used sophisticated spectroscopic instruments and involved little conventional chemistry, mostly to meticulously purify the materials under study. Combining these experimental results with quantum theory led to important conclusions regarding the electronic structure of molecules and a host of fascinating phenomena occurring in the excited state of molecules. As we were required to attend weekly departmental seminars, I had many occasions to hear several talks on these exciting topics. At first, I understood only a fraction of what I heard but I got the gist of it. However, I was intimidated by the mathematical language used and realized that I must develop my background to excel in this field. I knew then that quantum chemistry and spectroscopy (the study of light absorption and emission) was the field of my interest, and that the research group of Dr. Michael Kasha, or MK, as he was often addressed, was the group that I wanted to join. The fact that MK had a charismatic personality enhanced my desire to make a move.

My Egyptian companion was quite happy with his research assignment and his Professor, of Polish ethnic background, had a flamboyant personality. Since he had his MSc degree from Alexandria and had many years of research behind him, my companion had no problem fitting in quickly in spite of the fact that his English left a lot to be desired. His work required extensive chemical preparations involving various techniques such as distillation, extraction and crystallization. One might say "real" chemistry.

After being taken off the tadpole project, I was assigned to another biochemistry project that was more to my liking. I had to do an extensive search in the library. The great help that I received from different librarians made me respect this profession. They took special pleasure in helping students at a time when no computers or even photocopying machines were available. I had to take notes, which consumed lots of time but forced me to read and understand the material on the spot. My professor was upset that I was not spending enough time in the laboratory. I guess he thought I was goofing off! His behavior reflected little trust and respect and made me very unhappy.

Flitman, another graduate student in the group, would spend long hours in the lab, but did poorly in course work that led him to drop out. However, he got the admiration of our professor who once told me that he wished that I would spend more time in the lab and that Flitman would spend more time in studying his courses. I discovered a new spectrophotometric technique that worked beautifully to the extent that my professor doubted my results and had a technician confirm them. For me, that was the last straw, and I decided to leave that lab somehow. Later, we got our research paper on this technique published in the prestigious Journal of the American Chemical Society, or JACS as most preferred to call it. I've realized by now that Americans are fond of abbreviations: P Chem, FSU, OK, JR, NSF, FBI, CIA, VIP, ASAP, TGIF, GI, MIT, and many more.

My frustration grew and manifested itself physically with heart palpitations, stomach aches and anxiety. I went to the doctor who told me that all the symptoms were psychosomatic and that I needed a break. Since the semester had ended, I decided to join an Iraqi acquaintance for a trip in southern Florida. I went to see my professor to inform him that I would be away on a trip for a week. He was not in his office so I left him a short note. Later I was told that he was furious, which was something I did not anticipate. During the trip I made up my mind: try to fulfill my dream by moving to Kasha's group and if this could not be achieved, then I would return to Egypt. The trip was enjoyable in spite of my companion who was boring and spoke very little. His interest in the trip was apparently to register that he had been in the places we visited rather than actually enjoying them. Aside from commercial aspects, it was very nice seeing Weeki Wachee Springs, Cyprus Gardens, being photographed with beautiful young women in special fancy dresses, and viewing the swimming pool that was the scene of synchronized swimming in the Esther Williams movies that fascinated me. We also visited Orlando, Clearwater and St. Petersburg, a nice tour of a good part of Florida. The trip served its purpose, allowing me to think clearly and reach my decision.

Upon my return to Tallahassee, I gathered my courage and went to Professor Michael Kasha's office and told him about my desire to join his group. I expected that he would request a review of my grades and ask about my background particularly in mathematics and physics. I was simply stunned when he told me there and then that he welcomed me in his group and that he would provide me with a research assistantship. When I told him of my weak math background, he assured me that this could easily be remedied by taking the necessary courses. I was simply thrilled, so I thanked him and made a request not to mention my transfer to his lab before first talking with my professor. He agreed. That was one of the greatest days of my life. I rushed to tell my three Egyptian chemistry colleagues. They were skeptical of my ability to succeed in such a difficult field, but that did not quench my excitement one bit.

The next difficult task was to talk to my current supervisor. MK had already told him when he met him at Mecca, the popular coffee shop across from campus. I went to his office and told him. He was so angry that he hit his head against an open drawer of his steel filing cabinet and blood oozed from it. I felt very bad and tried to help but his anger persisted. He told me of his offer of the fellowship in spite of bad relations between the US and Nasser. I argued that as a professor he ought to encourage me to pursue my research interests. He praised my research abilities and tried to convince me to continue in his lab, but I politely declined. He insisted that I finish an MSc degree, which I quickly accepted. I knew I could finish the work before the fall when I would move to MK's group. I was motivated to work extremely hard not only because of deadlines but also because my then fiancé, Soo Soo, would be arriving to join me in the end of August.

My enthusiasm was greatly enhanced as I looked forward to join MK's group and to start my married life with Soo Soo. I had a great incentive to work very hard to finish the research work necessary for the Master's degree to the point that I spent several nights in the lab. I moved out of the apartment which I shared with my Egyptian companion and rented a nice apartment near campus in a street which had many pecan trees

Soon after the arrival of Soo Soo and after a very short, but memorable, honeymoon in New York, we returned to Tallahassee. We immediately got involved in our student activities, her as an undergraduate and I as a graduate student. She was elated as a freshman, nowadays fresh woman, and became busy in her course work. She decided to major in Bacteriology which required several Chemistry courses that I helped her with. I too became very busy finishing the formalities of my MSc degree, in addition to course work to develop my background needed for quantum chemistry and spectroscopy courses.

I remember distinctly the first day when MK came to the tiny desk assigned to me and started to clean it with a towel. When I objected, he refused to give me the towel to do the cleaning myself explaining that his action was to welcome me in his group. A few days later when I was in my tiny office studying, he noted that it was Sunday, and insisted that I go home to enjoy the weekend with my beautiful, young wife. These small gestures left a profound effect on me. I felt that I was dealing with a true professor, a caring person and a scientist who treated his students with dignity and as future scientists, not as an investment or laborers. That endeared him to me, made me work even harder and I will never forget that. His ways were in remarkable contrast to my earlier professor who demanded a schedule of my activities, which completely turned me off.

Finally, I achieved my dream of becoming a member of MK's group. I was enjoying the early period of finding my way in the lab and getting to know other members of the group, senior students who were about to graduate. Some were more helpful than others in breaking me in by teaching me how to operate instruments, purify solvents or understand some course material. There was a new student like myself who shared with me a real tiny room with a sliding door, so tiny that one had to move inward to allow the other person to leave his small desk. There was an Italian postdoctoral fellow who spoke little English with a heavy accent. He was clumsy with instruments but turned out to be an excellent theoretical chemist. Identifying one's real interest and abilities is not a straight forward task, and sometimes it involves trial and error. Another graduate student confessed his racist attitude and how he had advanced to the point of conversing with me! He was kind hearted, but, unfortunately, he was brought up to dislike and fear people of color and non- European foreigners. He used to tell me half jokingly, "I hate you basically". Frankly, I did not take him seriously and even liked him. There were also part time technicians and a secretary. This was the group that I spent four exciting years with.

In time, I began to pursue research projects suggested by MK and develop ideas of my own. I was fascinated by the concept of energy transfer when the energy of an excited molecule is transferred to a neighboring molecule. I chose a simple system and designed a set of experiments to show that energy transfer occurred unequivocally. It all worked beautifully, MK and I co-authored a paper published in the prestigious Journal of Chemical Physics. What a thrill! When I presented the work at the Spectroscopy meeting held annually in Columbus, Ohio, I was very nervous and could hear my heart beating. When I finished, a prominent scientist from the University of Chicago praised my work profusely. He was particularly impressed by the scientific methodology used, a subject that was one of his prime interests. I was extremely pleased especially when other scientists congratulated me. I must say that research ideas do not arise from a vacuum. I was influenced by the exciting work of a German scientist, Dr. Theodore Forster, who presented his work at a conference in Brookhaven National Labs. MK had most of the group fly to attend the meeting. It was my first flight ever and it was on the unsafe Electra turbojet that was later grounded. It was MK's generosity and his interest in developing us as scientists that gave me such a unique opportunity.

My life as a graduate student was not all work; it included lots of other types of fun. At the annual meeting in Columbus, we met several interesting young scientists, went to restaurants and bars with them and exchanged gossip as well as scientific ideas. One story I still remember was about one well known professor who had a graduate student who was smart, but fell in love with his mentor's wife and ran away with her. A year later, he wanted to return to finish his research work which he loved. The professor accepted the student back telling him, "It is more difficult to replace a good graduate student than to replace a wife".

Those Great Scientists and Their Great Discoveries

One of the great privileges that I had in being a part of MK's group was meeting well known scientists either in his laboratory or in conferences that he provided us with funds to attend. Some of them gave memorable lectures at FSU. We knew the names of those scientists well, and often read about their great achievements in text books, and, thus, they had a mythical aura about them. Many of them received a Nobel Prize. One received two and, ironically, a few of them never received this most prestigious prize. Meeting such great minds was exciting, yet seeing them face to face, listening to their lectures and talking to them removed some of the aura surrounding them in our minds. Suddenly they became real people rather than imaginary ones. This did not diminish my respect and admiration for any of them or reduce the significance of their achievements in my mind. Nevertheless, my perception had certainly undergone a major transformation. Actually, this is true when one meets any celebrity for the first time.

An added pleasure was to discover distinctive attributes of their personalities and amusing aspects of their characters. One learns that one's perception of another person is dynamic rather than static and depends on what is revealed of the person's character, as well as the dynamic evolution of both personalities of the observer and the observed.

MK was the student receiving his Ph D with G. N. Lewis before his sudden death. That made Lewis my "grandfather", scientifically speaking. The lobby of the Chemistry Department at Michigan State University, where I later taught as a professor, had a large framed genealogy of its entire faculty which showed the scientific "family" tree of each faculty member. Mine started with Kasha followed by Lewis then by a Nobel Laureate, Theodore W. Richards, and continued upwards through six French scientists, including Antoine L. Lavoisier (1743-1794) and ending with Guillaume Francois Rouelle (1703-1770). So my French line is very strong. Lavoisier was the French chemist who established the law of conservation of mass. Unfortunately for him and for science as well, he was also a tax collector for the monarchy. He was guillotined in 1764 during the French Revolution. The French judge stated, "The Republic needs neither scientists nor chemists". One and a half years later the French Government acknowledged that he was falsely convicted: too late! One famous mathematician said, "It took them only an instant to cut off his head, but France may not produce another like him in a century."

Gilbert Newton Lewis's contribution to modern chemistry is colossal. Every student who took a course in general chemistry in high school or as a university freshman would recognize the name. Lewis was the faculty advisor to several scientists who later received the Nobel Prize, like Melvin Calvin and Glenn T Seaborg. Like MK, Lewis ironically did not receive the Nobel Prize. MK admired Lewis greatly and described him as a very modest man who did not go to conferences very often and shunned the public relations game in pursuit of the prize. Visiting the laboratory where that great scientist worked during my stay in Berkeley as a visiting Professor in later years had a special meaning to me.

MK transmitted an exciting atmosphere in the group and promoted ethical professorial values. I would call MK "Mr. Triplet" because he identified a molecular state called the triplet, which is responsible for the long lived light emission called phosphorescence. MK went on to make several discoveries and contributions to earn him the title of "founder of modern molecular photochemistry". His interests were varied. One time, he asked me to examine ancient Egyptian instruments that were in Cairo Museum. I was able to get permission to handle these ancient instruments. One could imagine the awe I felt when touching them. He also got me interested in studying the spectra of indigo extracted from ancient Egyptian dyed cloth. Since marine indigo has bromine atoms, the spectrum is distinct from Nile indigo and thus one could determine exactly when Egyptians imported and used marine indigo used by the Romans.

It was simply fun to work with MK and his group. There was rarely a dull moment. On the personal level, MK was a kind and charming man, a fantastic storyteller - never mind the exaggeration here and there. He would tell us stories regarding his house on the lake, Berkeley days and G. N. Lewis, his venture to redesign guitars and his not quite successful attempts to play it. The group included a variety of individuals from the flamboyant Irish who became the chancellor of LSU, to the quiet thoughtful and philosophical Indian scientist. It included the blunt postdoctoral as well as the Southerner who was struggling with his own racism. The group included an Australian who became Professor at Melbourne University. Recently he had a tour visiting his friends in the States, including myself, and his health was failing. My family was happy to meet my old friend. He had babysat our child Gigi who is now a Professor of Internal Medicine at George Washington University. After his return to Melbourne he died. Soheir and I were very sad and will always have nice memories of him. Stewart Strickler, whom I shared for several years perhaps the smallest room in graduate school, went on to become the chairman of the Chemistry department in Boulder Colorado. Recently my grandson went on a Bike tour from DC to Colorado where he called him. As always Stew was friendly even though he was in hospital for a bout of pneumonia. There was also Mostafa who finished his PhD with a colleague named Wolfgang who committed suicide by taking his yacht out to the sea and kept going! Mostafa joined the group as a postdoctoral. Later he joined the Chemistry department at U. of California, Los Angeles. He became the Editor of the prestigious Journal of Physical Chemistry. Recently he received the Presidential Medal for his scientific achievements. There were other students, post doctors, technicians, secretaries, including the old timer Mrs. Hargrett, lab assistants, guest scientists. What an exciting group. We had coffee every morning, which gave me the chance to speak about my new experiments particularly when a discovery was made.

A great scientist and philosopher who I had the pleasure of knowing and the privilege of becoming friends with was Dr. John R. Platt. As a matter of fact, I am borrowing the title of this chapter from the title he used for a book he published in the Sixties. John was an atypical scientist. A stereotypical scientist has a narrow interest focused solely on his specific field of specialization, little social skill and a limited involvement in other aspects of life. This contradicts my experience that brought me together with several scientists that were jovial and have a wide range of interests in art, archeology, music, history, travel and different cultures. John was certainly one of them. He was full of life and had a wide circle of friends, scientists and otherwise. He expressed his feelings freely and openly. I remember him showing me a wild photograph hanging on the wall of his apartment in Ann Arbor, Michigan of his gorgeous goddaughter posing in a dancing gesture while completely nude. She must have been in her early twenties. His love of science, joy in promoting young scientists and new ideas, and his genuine adherence to the ideal of being a "professor" earned him lots of respect and love.

Platt was always interested in scientific methodology as it applies not only to physics and chemistry, but also to biological and social sciences. These days, I wish that politicians, rulers and decision makers in general would benefit from the genre of scientific methodology advocated by him.

From my own experience I find this to be true. Examples that come to mind include the case of polywater. Russian scientists claimed the existence of a new form of water that is more stable than regular water. The peculiarity that polywater could only be prepared from freshly drawn glassware apparently did not alert other scientists that something is wrong. The scientific sin committed was that no elementary analysis was done. After several months of wasted effort, when analysis was finally performed, the silly puzzle was cleared - polywater was essentially junk silica from the freshly drawn glass with some regular water. Several years later, two scientists claimed that they achieved the fusion of hydrogen atoms to form helium at room temperature thereby releasing a tremendous amount of energy, the same process that occurs in a hydrogen bomb. It did not take a genius to know that this was impossible because cold fusion defies well established facts regarding the huge energy barrier that must be surmounted to fuse two atoms of hydrogen. Yet, several other scientists in different parts of the world, including one in Kuwait, claimed they too had achieved cold fusion. That was a hoax. A well designed experiment that disproved such claims was later performed at MIT.

FSU had its share of brilliant scientists other than MK. Sidney Fox, who was on my Masters degree committee, showed that amino acids can spontaneously form small peptides and later those could form microspheres and perhaps protocells that can divide, which suggested that these steps could constitute the origins of life on Earth. Beidler was studying the molecular mechanism of taste. Chopin made valuable contributions to the field of radiation chemistry. He was a student of Glen Seaborg, the discoverer of some new elements including one named after him, seaborgium.

There were sad moments too. At FSU, Professor James Fisher, who was also on my Masters degree committee and studied the development of chick embryos, was shot dead by a Japanese student who had just failed his examination. Also, a young scientist who had just joined the faculty and who taught me quantum chemistry drowned while diving in Wakulla Springs near Tallahassee.

In general, however, I had lots of fun during my graduate school years. I remember break times when we four Egyptians met around the Coke machine on the third floor searching desperately for one penny to add to the nickel in order to have a coke. Our laughter attracted attention and curiosity. Another funny moment happened one weekend when a partly drunk physics professor, who had obviously mistaken which floor he was on, was getting out of the Ladies Room swearing that there were urinals before! Also, jokes about two professors who taught different sections of a math course were frequently circulated by students like "Flunk it with Plunkett" and "Get it made with Wade". When the tall physics building was built it was labeled by some students as "Plyler's Last Erection". Plyler was the old Physics Department Chairman. The Institute of Molecular Biophysics, IMB, now called Kasha Laboratory, was nicknamed IBM for its resemblance to the old computer punch cards.

Such was and is the excitement of science.

EPISODE TWENTY-THREE:
Cambridge: Yankee Country

As I was finishing up my Masters degree at FSU, John Platt offered me a generous post doctoral fellowship at the University of Chicago to pursue research on topics of my choosing. John advocated the need of alternative hypotheses coupled with strong inference to drive good science and to speed up its progress. Platt often warned of being too attached to one hypothesis and the danger of pressing facts to make them fit a theory and, thus, substituting faith for science.

I accepted his offer as it would give me a great opportunity to widen my interest and background. Knowing that another well known theoretical scientist, Robert S. Mulliken, and his group were also in the same department was an added attraction, even though I had negative impressions about Chicago. John Platt and Mulliken did not like each other. As a matter of fact, John called him "my friendly enemy", but they were courteous to each other. I did not see any problem in my anticipated and desired interaction with the Mulliken group.

Mulliken was among those we interacted with at the previous Columbus meetings. He later received a Nobel Prize for his successful application of quantum mechanics to the electronic structure of molecules. His lectures were not exciting. In fact, they required extra concentration and energy to follow. He tended to divert from the main points to give several footnotes that were distracting. He also had a dry sense of humor. Once at dinner at a restaurant in Columbus, he could not find a place to put his papers and notes so he put them momentarily over his head. Once I was taking a short flight with him when he made a remark to the stewardess to sarcastically point out an apparent contradiction in the safety procedures. She started to explain to him the obvious in great detail. Little did she know that she was speaking to one of the greatest minds alive who was merely trying in his odd way to be comical. Nevertheless, I found him to be a likeable, kind old man whom I admired and respected greatly.

When my family was all set to go to Chicago, our plans suddenly changed. John decided to go to MIT to spend a sabbatical there, and gave me the choice of joining him or going to Chicago. I decided that it would be exciting to go to Cambridge and be in the great intellectual atmosphere of MIT and Harvard. The absence of a research lab at my disposal made me decide to do theoretical work. I would also be joined by another young postdoctoral scientist, Dr. David Kearns, who received his doctorate at Berkeley in photoconductivity with Melvin Calvin.

We packed our stuff, including what proved to be junk, and left Tallahassee and headed north in our green Dodge. It was not easy to leave. I had been with our research group for several years with lots of memories, mostly pleasant, and we were leaving many friends. As always, we were certain that we would continue communicating, but in reality that did not happen except for a short while.

After a long trip, we finally arrived in Boston. My Egyptian friend at Alexandria, Samir Hanna, whom I was hoping would be my companion at FSU was studying at MIT. He helped us find a place to spend a few nights. It was a large classical New England house with many rooms and tens of people. Soon after, we quickly found a small apartment at Mass Avenue conveniently located near MIT. We moved in quickly since we had planned to spend the summer at Woods Hole in Cape Cod. I was invited to spend most of the summer at the nearby labs of a prominent scientist, Dr. Albert Szent-Gyorgi Von Nagryapolt. That was a treat both scientifically and recreationally. We rented a nice but expensive apartment in Falmouth and quickly established a routine of research work, swimming at stony Falmouth beaches and socializing in the evening. That was a nice cocktail of activities, which included Gigi, our delightful two year old daughter.

Of course one main highlight of that period was interacting with Szent-Gyorgi. We chatted a lot and covered various topics including his many adventures. His early years were in Hungary, during a turbulent time, in the eye of the storm of World War I. We often joined him at the beach where we noticed that he had a peculiar scar on his arm. I learned later that it was the result of a self inflicted bullet wound that allowed him to leave a war he detested. That was his unorthodox, perhaps crazy, way to avoid the war, although his method was not quite unique. In Egypt many peasants cut a finger to avoid being drafted into the army. At Cambridge, England, he made history and came to impact every individual forever by isolating a substance from adrenal gland tissue that was nothing other than Vitamin C. As if that was not enough, his contributions continued, particularly in the area of what is called bioenergetics, the understanding of the details of the cellular combustion process that contributed to the Krebs Cycle. He advanced our understanding of the molecular mechanism of muscle contractions, growth, and the biochemistry of cancer, including the possibility that free radicals (very active chemical species) may be a cause of cancer.

Szent-Gyorgi was vehemently antifascist, not in words but in practice. He joined the Hungarian resistance. Because Hitler personally wanted him arrested, he spent some time as a fugitive from the Gestapo. Before ending up at Woods Hole Marine Laboratories, he was elected as a member of the Hungarian Parliament, considered as a candidate for the presidency after World War II and later escaped Communist rulers. He was known to hate submitting research grant applications with all their required details of plans of work and budget allocations. His rebellious and flamboyant personality, love of life, women, swimming, food and music made him a sort of gypsy scientist. I remember his advice to me not to return to Egypt given the limited research facilities there. Instead, he urged me to pursue an academic research career in the US, advice I ultimately did not take. When he died in 1986 at the age of nearly ninety, I eulogized him in my class at Alexandria University. I simply admired the man and his character. I greatly appreciated and valued his contributions to science. He was not your average Nobel Laureate, and stood out for his brilliance, broad knowledge and power of scientific intuition.

I began to be immersed in theoretical research after we returned to Cambridge at the end of the summer. David Kearns joined me in the research that eventually led to two publications in a prestigious scientific journal. John Platt did not join us in the authorship of the papers even though he was the source of our funds. A mark of a true scientist is to be a co-author only if he or she contributed to the work. I enjoyed the company of David who had a young daughter of a similar age as my daughter Gigi. Both our families socialized and went to picnics together, especially during the fall when the trees exploded in a remarkable display of colors. He later became a Professor at the University of California, San Diego.

At Harvard, I met another great scientist, Dr. George Wald, who received the Nobel Prize in Physiology and Medicine for his important and elegant work on vision. He and his group extracted rhodopsin, the visual pigment from the rod cells of the retina, and determined their light absorption characteristics. Later, he measured the absorption properties of cone cells. He stood out as a rare example of a well known scientist who articulated bold views on political and social issues, bold because they were out of the main stream thinking at the time as many great stands are. He not only opposed the crazy nuclear arms race and the Vietnam War, but he also participated in public demonstrations against both. He worked for the release of Russian activists, such as Andrei Sakharov, and did the same for the US hostages taken in Iran in 1979.

The excitement in Cambridge was perpetual. That year, 1961, Melvin Calvin, David's former professor, received the Nobel Prize in Chemistry. He came to Harvard to share in teaching a special graduate course in the Biology Department in which several scientists also participated, including Kasha, Kearns and myself. Some Chinese paper in San Francisco had leaked the news about the award, so when Calvin gave his lecture in the course he already knew and used the occasion to practice his Nobel address. He would change some of his statements and would throw the chalk in his hand when he was not satisfied with what he was saying! Although that made the talk hard to enjoy, he was a Noble Laureate recipient so I suppose he was entitled to such behavior. Several years later in 1991 when I was a visiting Professor at the University of California, Berkeley, I saw him whenever he came to the Physical Chemistry Department luncheon. In fact, I sometimes walked back to the Department with him holding his hand to help him up hill.

Calvin and Wald worked on two vital pigments associated with two phenomena that are central to our lives, vision and photosynthesis. Calvin discovered the chemical steps involved in the transformation of carbon dioxide to starch. The crucial phenomenon of photosynthesis that occurs in green plant leaves is a remarkably efficient natural process to store solar energy. The complete understanding of this process would be a prelude for utilizing solar energy as the cleanest form of energy production.

At MIT, there was a lot of excitement focused on lasers and DNA. There were new studies on the structure of these marvelous molecules that carry the code of life from one generation to the next, some call it "The Book of Life". New solid lasers were invented and in 1960 Ali Javan, an Iranian scientist at MIT, invented the gas laser. Every time I passed by his laboratory, which was located in the same building as my office, I saw the bustling activity and sensed the excitement on the faces of young scientists working in his group. Lasers' predecessors, masers, were discovered earlier in 1954. As a matter of fact, the inventor, Dr. Charles Townes, was at MIT in 1961 as its Provost. As most serious scientists like to avoid administrative work, he resigned before the end of the year and went back fully to research at Berkeley. He received his Nobel Prize in 1964. Both devices, masers and lasers were based on an old article by Einstein published much earlier in 1917. The paper distinguished spontaneous emission from stimulated emission with the latter having the unique characteristic of coherence. Obviously, it was not experimentally feasible for a long time to generate stimulated emission, the "se" in masers and lasers.

It is amusing to recall an article in a local newspaper that called lasers "a discovery searching for an application". Can you imagine that lasers were void of applications in 1961?! Nowadays, without knowing what the word means, millions of people all over the world know of one or more application of lasers, such as security devices or the repair of retinal detachment. Of course, there are wide applications of lasers in various areas of medicine, engineering, entertainment, communication and, unfortunately, the military. More importantly, lasers are a highly potent research tool in a wide range of scientific research fields. So much for searching for applications. Scientists welcome useful applications of their newly discovered devices, but they do not worry if an application is not apparent in the horizon. It is more than enough if they solve an academic problem or lead to a further scientific insight.

I enjoyed my theoretical research, but I greatly missed designing experiments that test ideas and theories. One time, I was walking back to our apartment near MIT late at night, and my mind was deeply immersed in aspects of my research. Routinely, I entered the apartment and started taking off my clothes in the dark as my wife and young daughter were asleep and I did not want to disturb them. As my eyes started to adapt to the darkness, I realized that I was in the wrong apartment! I was so scared, so I quietly collected my clothes and shoes and sneaked out. I looked up and down the staircase to identify the floor and as fast as I could I entered our apartment. "How could my key open the wrong apartment right above us?", I asked myself. What would have happened if I jumped in the bed as I usually do? It all sounded like a funny movie, but at the time it was not funny at all. I was so nervous I had to awaken my wife to tell her what happened.

As time for departure to Egypt approached, my scientist friends repeatedly advised me to stay in the US. Even though my mind was set to return to Alexandria University, I started to reevaluate my decision as their argument was sound and logical. Certainly, there would not be adequate research facilities at Alexandria and the environment would not be as conducive to coming up with creative ideas as it would be in the vibrant research atmosphere in good American universities. All that was true and, logically, I believed that I ought to stay in the US if I based my decision on the goal of solely pursuing my career. However, there were other goals to pursue that were equally important. My dream was to be part of an endeavor to promote excellence in research and teaching at Alexandria University and other Egyptian institutions. I was convinced that this goal was achievable once the political vision and commitment were there. The question remained whether such commitment really existed in Egypt.

One day, I was invited to a job interview at a newly established Laboratory for research at IBM in San Jose, California. I was tempted to go and lecture at San Jose and see my Italian friend who became an important member of the research group there doing theoretical computations of the electronic structures of molecules. However, I had to be honest and declined the invitation on the ground that I am returning to Egypt. Nevertheless, I was asked to visit and I was delighted to go. Everything went well, and I enjoyed the trip thoroughly. My ego got a boost when I was given an open, signed offer to join at a later time if I changed my mind. There were also available opportunities at a number of prestigious universities but I had to agonize and declined to explore them.

It was winter in Cambridge and the snow started in earnest. At first, it was delightful to experience snow falling and snow-covered streets, but quickly it became a huge hassle to park especially when piles of snow surrounded the perimeter of the spot. An opportunity arose to go to Florida to attend the Winter School of Quantum Chemistry at Sanibel Island. Not only was that a great opportunity to attend an intense, advanced seminar on the subject from several of the masters of the field, but it was also a great spot to spend two weeks in the sunshine of Southern Florida. I must have felt guilty to leave my family in Cambridge during the harsh winter, but my main motivation was to strengthen my background in quantum chemistry. The organizer of the Winter School was a well known Swedish scientist, Dr. Per-Olov Lowdin, who had organized a similar school each summer in Uppsala, Sweden. Although I enjoyed the lectures and the swimming, I did not feel comfortable socially since I did not know most of the participants.

Back again in Cambridge, I continued doing my research, and attending seminars at Harvard and MIT. I met several interesting scientists there, among them Dr. Blout who was involved in developing a colored Polaroid camera, which seemed a formidable task at the time, but it was done.

My wife worked in the lab of a famous biochemist so we had to take our daughter Gigi to a babysitter. During that time, we met B.F. Skinner at Harvard who conducted experiments that showed how crucial the touch of mothers is to the normal development of baby monkeys. He was highly impressed with the intelligence of Gigi. When he asked her what is in the air, she responded with clear enunciation "oxygen molecules". Likewise, she said "spectroscopy" in response to a question as to what I do. She was in the most delightful stage of her development enjoying the snow, the Charles River and Alvin & the Chipmunks' songs.

We also enjoyed the company of John Platt. A few years later he and his wife Ann visited us in Egypt and we spent a great time. I remember particularly a Nile "fluka" ride and an evening on the roof of the Nile Hilton where we watched a celebrated belly dancer (Samia Gamal) perform. John was fascinated by her artistic dance and as he told me the sensual gestures on her face. We saw each other several times in different cities. I was very saddened when he died of a brain tumor at the age of 74.

In the Fall of 1962, many Egyptians came to study for their doctorates at MIT or Harvard. The Egyptian Government had an ambitious plan to send hundreds of selected students to study in Europe, the United States, and what was then the Soviet Union, and to specialize in various advanced fields of science, engineering and economics to help in the development of Egypt. About ten Egyptian students lived in our apartment building. Most of them were of my age or older even though I had already finished my PhD. I often visited them in their apartments. There were always lively discussions centered on our role when we get back home. Priorities of development and the role of science and scientific research were the focus of our concerns. Discussions were muted when it came to the then Egyptian President Gamal Abdel Nasser. Criticism was forbidden, although it was self imposed for fear of being reported. Unfortunately, some of the students acted as informants. Officials of the Egyptian Education Bureau in Washington DC were rumored to have organized a network of such informants, who acted as the "Guardians of the Revolution". Time would prove that most, if not all were opportunists.

After Nasser's death in 1970, many continued to play the same role, but in an opposite ideological direction. It took some time to realize that in all societies including in democracies, self interest rather than principles or convictions guide the actions of the vast majority. This is valid in spite of the short-lived appearance of authenticity. Some of the vehement self-proclaimed Nasserites became enthusiastic supporters of Sadat and later Mubarak. Moreover, some joined the chorus of condemning Nasser. These sudden switches in beliefs and loyalties are not uncommon. In fact, I dare say that nowadays it has become the norm.

In Cambridge, I witnessed the budding of what many now call Islamic Fundamentalism, which is more accurately a form of a backward and distorted ideology shaped and financed by Gulf Arab States that are rich in oil and poor in culture - also described as "Petro-Islam". The Director of the Islamic Center in Washington DC came to lecture at Harvard University. Among the attendants was Gibbs, a noted scholar on Islam. Privately, the Director clearly expressed that he was personally intimidated by Gibbs. He obviously had ample reason to feel this discomfort as he did not possess the scholarship or the intellect that Gibbs had. That did not mean that I agreed with everything said or written about Islam by Orientalists such as Gibbs. Quite the contrary, I disagree with basic issues of their discourse. Nevertheless, the lecture was an embarrassment to me and others. The Director's opening line was, as I remember clearly, "all of us are mentally sick and psychologically disturbed". He was referring to the human need for God's salvation and help.

At that time, I was probing the utility of political Islam before I was convinced of the danger of theological statehood. I met a Jewish woman who converted to Islam and changed her name to Gameela, which means beautiful, Although she was anything but that, what really repelled me from her was her fanatic attitude, which went beyond the expected degree of fanaticism when one adopts a new belief or theory.

While our stay in Cambridge was rich and enjoyable, such joy was tainted a little with the mental tension of the repeated reevaluation of the decision to go back to Alexandria University, especially since my wife was not enthusiastic about that decision. We will always remember these wonderful days in Cambridge and surroundings, the colorful foliage, the snow, walking along the Charles River, shopping in the Italian Market, visiting the Science Museum, and attending concerts, exciting science seminars and public lectures. I particularly enjoyed a series of lectures given by Nelson

Rockefeller on Federalism. The vibrant intellectual atmosphere in Cambridge was certainly something else. We had the opportunity to travel a bit in New England, visiting Cape Cod, the beautiful rocky beaches of Maine and lush, green Vermont. A truly wonderful experience.

EPISODE TWENTY-FOUR:

The Return

We started planning our return to Alexandria in earnest. We drew up a shopping list which included appliances and other household items. Shopping became a priority, especially for Soheir since I never liked shopping. We ordered our first brand new car, a sky blue Chevrolet Impala, but we did not use it to see the USA as Dinah Shore had suggested, but to take it back to Egypt. Unfortunately, we had to sell it since we could not afford it and we needed additional money to settle and to supplement our monthly incomes. Also, I did not feel comfortable driving a fancy car at a time when car importation was severely restricted.

We finally packed all of our stuff, including my fancy stereo system, and rented a U-Haul. I drove to New York and arranged for the shipment of the appliances. We were leaving by ship as the Education Bureau restricted our paid return to travel by ship. We did not mind as this made it easier to take all our belongings with us. In fact, we looked forward to the ocean crossing, as well as the several stops the ship, Leonardo de Vinci, was scheduled to make at Casablanca, Palma de Majorca, Naples and, finally, Venice, where we were to take another ship to Alexandria. Gigi was very excited to be on an ocean liner.

An unexpected problem arose when we were clearing customs which dampened our excitement. An IRS official who was a Chinese-American woman claimed that we had to pay a few thousand dollars in back taxes. What a disaster that would have been, I tried to convince her that we were

ASHRAF EL-BAYOUMI | 169

on fellowships as graduate students and we were explicitly exempted from taxes. She was adamant and insisted that we cannot leave until we pay what would have been most of our savings. Finally, I came up with the idea that she should call the head of the Chemistry Department at FSU and ask him. She reluctantly agreed, but would not let me talk to him. He confirmed that the tax exemption I used was completely legitimate and it did apply to all graduate students. What a relief. She finally signed the necessary papers that showed that all due taxes were indeed paid. Frankly, I felt that she was kind of disappointed with the outcome!

Finally, we were on board the ship and a nice room was assigned to us. An Egyptian friend who was completing his doctorate in economics at Harvard came to bid us farewell. To our delight, the long crossing of the Atlantic Ocean began. After weeks of running around, shopping, packing, driving, and getting through customs, we were relaxing with nothing to do except chatting, reading and dreaming.

The Trip

The first short stop after the long Atlantic crossing was the beautiful city of Casablanca, which literally means the White House. It was a relief to be on land after many days at sea with no obligations, shopping or errands. However, that was a welcomed period to relax and reflect on our life experience in the US and to project our several expectations when we arrive in Egypt.

In Casablanca, we had the first taste of being in an Arab country since our departure several years ago. To hear Arabic and eat Arabic food and be surrounded with Arabic people induced a special feeling of being home once again. I would not know the impact of being in a culture so different from the American culture on a child less than three years old. I could only see the amazement of our daughter Gigi who was suddenly exposed to a multitude of new experiences. Her brain must have been so busy registering new scenes, different faces, strange tastes and unusual sounds. No wonder that a child's development undergoes a quantum leap and a remarkable jolt during the early years of life when the brain is still new.

It is difficult to imagine that this cheerful, beautiful city was once an important harbor for pirates. Now it is the base of the Moroccan Navy and is the largest port of Morocco. The French architectural style was evident to us. Beautiful mosques and traditional Arab buildings reminded us that we are in an Arab country. We were also conscious of the history of the city during the French colonial period, and the rioting of the population against the French, which peaked after World War II. We were reminded with the obvious similarity of our Arab history as we also rioted against British rule in Egypt during the late Forties. High school students like me demonstrated against the British. Such demonstrations were often met with violence by both the British soldiers and Egyptian police.

One cannot be in Casablanca without some scenes, memorable phrases or tunes from Humphrey Bogart and Ingrid Bergman's film Casablanca flashing in one's mind. Our short stay was delightful, including the food. Elaborate Moroccan cuisine has its unique taste and uses almonds and sweets with its main meat and chicken dishes. We visited Casablanca several times after this brief introduction and were never disappointed.

Our next stop was the Spanish island of Palma de Majorca. Gigi was quite amused by the horse carriage ride. I always had a soft spot for such rides, the rhythmic sound of the horse and palm trees. If that does not put anyone in a romantic mood nothing else will. Palma, under Arabic rule for several centuries, enjoyed a long period of peaceful coexistence between the Christian city and the Muslim rulers in Spain. It was inescapable to us to see the similarities of our own features and those of the islanders.

Back on the ship, we returned to the routine we got used to. The next day we were in Naples. The shouts, quarrels and the vitality of the people reminded us that we were in Italy. This was my second visit to Naples with the first being almost seven years earlier on my way to the States. We took a taxi to Pompeii and neither my wife nor Gigi enjoyed the visit. It was very hot and Gigi was not particularly interested in seeing old stones as she put it then. We were looking forward to our next exciting stop, Venice

I associated Venice with charm, romance and art, and when I finally arrived, my expectations were exceeded. A city of hundreds of bridges and canals, Venice is indeed most charming. We spent two nights in a cozy hotel by one of the canals. A gondola ride was delightful, and I had brief imaginary romantic moments thanks to the creative power of the mind. We visited the famous Piazza Saint Marco, where Gigi was mesmerized by the many pigeons.

Ausonia was a faster air conditioned ship which made our last leg of the trip more comfortable. Members of the crew were friendly and delightful. The Italian captain of the ship invited our Gigi alone for supper at his table where she behaved like a young lady. It is amazing how children exhibit all what they have learned at unexpected moments. Her photos with the captain clearly reflected a confident and relaxed individual who was having a great time. One memorable dinner on the boat was a fish meal. The cooked fish was displayed before being served and devoured. The spicy smell and the inviting appearance were matched by its taste. Mediterranean fish in my opinion is the tastiest fish anywhere.

We stopped at the very beautiful port city of Dubrovnik in Yugoslavia, which was then a united country with various ethnicities under the leadership of Josip Broz-Tito. Tito was widely admired for his heroic role as the guerilla leader of Yugoslav partisans who fought brilliantly against Nazis during World War II. Tito was also liked by Egyptians for his support of Egypt and his close friendship with Nasser. We enjoyed walking around the old city with its walls and the beautiful turquoise sea water, and we felt the serenity of strolling without the noise or the pollution of cars. Gigi in particular felt the freedom of uninhibited running around. It was more like walking in a fairy tale story along the Yellow Brick Road.

We proceeded to the tip of Italy where the quiet city of Brindisi lies. The quietness of the city was in sharp contrast to its violent history, a history filled with repeated conquests and destructive earthquakes. Like many other cities of the Mediterranean Sea, Brindisi had its share of conquests. It was conquered twice by the Byzantines, raided repeatedly by pirates and ruled by numerous powers: Normans, Naples, Venice, Spain and Austria. We walked along the road by the sea with its typical Mediterranean cafés. An incident reminded us that old habits do not die easily. Young men were flirting with Soheir, who was several months pregnant with our second child. One of them pinched her, a habit not rare in Egypt either. I remembered at once when I heard years ago a sudden scream of a woman while watching a movie in Alexandria. Lights were turned on and the city official who was among the viewers ordered the man arrested. There were no city officials walking near us in Brindisi, and we elected not to create a scene and walked away peacefully. The ship started its fast crossing of the Mediterranean towards beloved Alexandria.

All along the trip, especially during the last few days, we discussed our plans, expectations and our worries, including the personal, the academic and the public. I expected problems with the Alexandria University since I was several months beyond the deadline of my return. I also realized that adapting to the very different academic atmosphere and its unwritten rules and habits would not be easy. However, such issues did not worry me as much as the anticipated tensions with Soheir's family.

The relationship between Soheir and her mother turned sour after my mother-in-law visited us when Gigi was a few months old. We did not meet her expectations. While she probably envisioned that we lived in a luxury apartment, we lived in modest university housing. She imagined that we would be fancily dressed, having dazzling parties, and going to exotic places and dining in fancy restaurants, the kind of image projected in American movies. Instead, our life then was mostly hard work and simple pleasures. There were a few picnics and occasional steak dinners at a fancy restaurant in Tallahassee, the Silver Slipper, but that fell quite short of my mother-in-law's expectations. We dressed casually and I often had pants with holes caused by chemicals. At that time the silly fad of having pants torn at the knees was not invented yet. We tried hard to make her visit pleasant and we planned to take her for a trip around Florida. Unfortunately, she left earlier than planned and was angry at us. She was probably extremely home sick. Unfortunately, she exaggerated negative incidents to justify her sudden departure. The sad thing was that this ruined our relation with my wife's parents until their death. Since I was the one who initiated the invitation of my mother in law, I consider that idea was one of the biggest blunders I had committed. I really thought that seeing her daughter after more than three years with a degree in bacteriology and a lovely child would be a tremendous source of happiness, but that was not the case. We tried hard many times to mend our relation through several relatives and friends, but to no avail. Soheir's mother was a charming woman, but she was very controlling and gave undue importance to appearances. Soheir's father was a very kind, loving man and he loved our children. However, he was forcibly deprived of the joy of interacting with his grandchildren. What a missed opportunity because I liked them both. Upon our return, we were expecting difficulties with Soheir's parents, but I did not imagine then that the relation would eventually be dead. My relief though was that I mistakenly thought that our marriage would have been in jeopardy if my in laws were in the same town.

We had a lot to do before we could settle in. On the top of the list was finding an apartment and furnishing it. Also, Soheir was expecting in a few months and we had to quickly identify a reliable gynecologist and a hospital for the delivery. There were burdens all right, but also there was the anticipated joy of returning and seeing my family after seven years of being away, the pride of achieving our educational goals and the pleasure of introducing our daughter, Gigi, to family and old friends. We expected that Soheir's family would not come to meet us at the port, which was both odd and sad, especially for Soheir.

Finally, after almost seven years for me and six for Soheir, Alexandria appeared on the horizon sparking a cocktail of strong emotions. I returned with my pregnant wife who received a B.Sc. degree in Bacteriology and our young daughter of almost three years old and I with a M.Sc. in Biochemistry and a PhD in Physical Chemistry, as well as a load of experiences and knowledge. There was my father and mother with several relatives including my three brothers and my sweet sister. My father could not hide his happiness and pride. However, Gigi stole the show. Actually, the welcoming party was smaller since there had been a sudden death in the family. Interestingly, a photo taken from behind members of my family, including three heavyweights, waving at us when the ship approached the dock became part of the brochure of the newly renovated Alexandria Port with three huge behinds that could easily be identified. As expected, my dear friend and grandfather was not present as his failing health kept him in Cairo. I was really saddened when I saw him later. I could not communicate with him except very briefly. Death has many definitions besides the cessation of breathing and heartbeats. Some are dead while still healthy, but some die when they lose their vibrant personalities and the beauty of their minds. He died several months later, but most of my tears were shed when I first saw him upon my return.

The romantic few days ended too quickly. First impressions were quite amusing. People appeared fatter and the streets narrower and people talked with much louder voices than in the US. On the other hand, some of my relatives thought that I was whispering. For them, my voice was low and they were worried that I may be sick. In a few days I proved that I was indeed in good health! We were reintroduced to Egyptian meals and to family issues including deaths, marriages, divorces and other events and problems. Gigi was not deprived from attention, including the flies that amused her. At that time, there were practically no flies in the US as DDT insecticide was in abundant use in spite of a few voices that warned of its danger.

I had to confront various issues all at once. Getting my luggage from customs was a burden for me because I did not know how to handle the indirect ways necessary to expedite the process. Thus, I was happy to delegate this burden to my younger brother who enjoyed such an activity. Going to college to settle problems connected with my delayed return from the US was another matter. I had to do that myself. Trying to mend our relations with my in-laws proved much more difficult. We were lucky in the task of finding a nice apartment as one of Soheir's uncles was quite helpful. Through his work as the Chairman of the Board of a large textile factory, he introduced me to a man who made his fortune from selling cloth. He was illiterate, but very bright, and, more importantly, he owned a fancy apartment building in the upscale district of Zizinia near the sea and across an old palace with a large garden. Furnishing the apartment was totally another task for we decided to have it custom made. We had specific ideas of what style we desired which was very different from available furniture. We searched for a good carpenter and we had a lucky break when we found La Maison, which had been owned by an Italian designer who left his furniture shop to his Egyptian apprentice.

As we slowly settled in Alexandria, our second daughter, Mona, was born and we adapted to the new style of life. It was enjoyable in many ways, walking by the sea along the corniche, and having a fresh fish meal at a Greek restaurant, Petro, by the sea not far from our apartment. Sometimes we went to Abu Kir a small town near Alexandria to have equally tasty roasted fish. We always remembered that Abu Kir was the sight of the victory of Admiral Nelson over the French Navy at the time when the British and the French were competing to occupy Egypt. Several battle ships are still sunk in the bay. The naval battle at Abu Kir was detrimental to the ambitions of Napoleon and the French. It eventually forced the French to leave Egypt, although Napoleon had escaped earlier by slipping away from the British Navy.

We bought a small used car which was convenient for us with two children, even though public transportation and taxi service were good. We occasionally traveled by car to Cairo to visit the family. We often visited the San Stefano Hotel by the sea with a lovely garden and an open-air movie theater, which was very convenient as it was only a few blocks from our apartment. A French patisserie in the back of the hotel was an attractive stop to have pieces of delicious gateau. Our financial situation was good and my salary as a Lecturer (Assistant Professor) was complemented by supervising science classes at the English Girls College where Gigi and later Mona attended kindergarten, and Soheir taught science. The atmosphere in the school was very nice. The garden, the swimming pool, the morning tea ritual, order and cleanliness were all very attractive to us.

As expected, I also faced many problems back at Alexandria University. The senior professor of physical chemistry with whom I started doing research before leaving for the States became quite antagonistic to me. One major reason perhaps was that I specialized in the modern field of quantum chemistry and molecular spectroscopy, which was far from his classical field of solution chemistry. That also made me independent of him, which is in contrast to common expectations at the college. His PhD student had just graduated and he wanted to promote him ahead of me in spite of my seniority. Eventually, the head of the department intervened on my behalf. This further poisoned my relationship with the senior professor and continued to be a source of tension with him. I wish that at the time I understood the difficulty of adjustments at various junctures in life such as when a former student becomes an independent scientist. The same can be said about other relationships, especially that between a young mother and her newly independent married daughter. These transitions demand psychological preparations, as well as painful adaptations.

Hopes and realities quickly clashed as far as research facilities were concerned. I had to compromise my research aspirations and at the same time to struggle to obtain modern equipment. That task proved futile since the political leadership was not convinced with the central importance of basic research and its necessity for the applied research it promoted. The military background of the rulers and their lack of comfort with universities and professors fed this attitude. Economic reasons and the scarcity of hard currencies were also major obstacles. I decided to use every opportunity to travel abroad for conferences or short summer visits to keep updated and use the opportunity to avail myself of more sophisticated equipment. I succeeded two or three times during a five year period. In spite of all the difficulties, I did not regret my return as I was still determined and hopeful to change the situation.

Our life for the five years we spent in Alexandria was a cocktail of contradictory feelings. Frustration from not achieving what can be achieved because of unnecessary barriers, and satisfaction from being able to introduce a modern field of chemistry. Yet, there was the perpetually nagging problem with my in-laws, a problem I wrongly and naively thought solvable. However, the greatest frustration was related to the political atmosphere which was dominated by police security elements, including collaborators among members of the faculty and graduate students. In brief, hypocritical elements in the society floated to the top. Ironically, or more accurately logically, such elements proved to be a detriment to the regime and more importantly to the society.

Family life was serene with my wife and our three children - we later had a son, Amr, who added a lot to our happiness. Two of our kids got quality education at the English Girls College and all three were lucky to experience a healthy and enjoyable environment. We particularly enjoyed strolling by the sea where I would carry my children on my shoulders when they were very young and not heavy. Such was our life in our beautiful Alexandria. Our life in the States was also an enjoyable unforgettable learning experience.

After five years in Alexandria, we moved to the States ending at Michigan State University where I served as a Professor for nearly thirteen years. Soheir received a PhD in Medical Anthropology and taught at MSU, while our kids completed their education in excellent schools and universities in Michigan. Our experience during those years was full of events, joy as well as struggle. Writing about that has to be postponed for another time and another place!

And such was my exciting, eye-opening and often times comical adventure to Amreeka the Wonderland.

The End

CPSIA information can be obtained
at www.ICGtesting.com
Printed in the USA
LVOW08s0620191017
552968LV00008B/180/P